Classical World series

ATHENS UNDER THE TYRANTS

J.A. Smith

Bristol Classical Press

General Editor: John H. Betts

First published in 1989 by
Bristol Classical Press, 226 North Street, Bedminster, Bristol BS3 1JD

British Library Cataloguing in Publication Data

Smith, J.A.
    Athens under the tyrants – (Classical world series)
    1. Greece. Athens, ancient period
    I. Title
    938'.5

    ISBN 1-85399-116-3

ATHENS UNDER THE TYRANTS

Classical World series
(*Series Editor: Michael Gunningham*)

FOR JILL

Contents

List of Illustrations

Chapter 1
Homer and Heroes

An age of heroes

'Strive always to be best, my son, and to be superior to others'. With these words from his father echoing in his ears, the young Achilles set off to make his name in the Trojan War.

This was the ideal which inspired the heroes of Homer's two epic poems. In the *Iliad* Achilles was quite simply the best fighter at Troy, and expected to be honoured as such. When he was denied the reward which he believed he deserved, he refused to fight; and it was not until his close friend Patroklos had been killed that he returned to battle to salvage his honour and show that he was still the best warrior on the battlefield. Wily Odysseus, the hero of the *Odyssey*, strove throughout to get back home safely and outwit his enemies by fair means or foul. He regularly congratulated himself on how clever he had been and what fools his defeated enemies were.

Such unashamed self-satisfaction grates a little on the modern ear, attuned by centuries of Christianity to regard humility as a virtue. The Greeks, however, took it for granted, and at no time more than in the second half of the sixth century BC, the period roughly covered by this book. Aristocrats of this century were steeped in Homer's poetry, and had made the aims and ideals of Homer's heroes their own. They believed that their past was encapsulated in the Homeric epics, and therefore to seek to imitate these giants of old was as natural as breathing.

When they could not fulfil their aggressive ambition on the field of war they competed in the athletics stadium where, with their pride and satisfaction in winning, there went a remarkably callous indifference towards those who had been defeated.

> Through the back alleys they slink,
> Out of the way of their enemies –
> Disaster has bitten them.
>
> (*Pythian Ode* 8.86-7)

wrote the poet Pindar of losers in the Pythian Games.

1

Such was the competitive spirit which dominated sixth-century Greece; but time was running out for would-be heroes. Politically, the Greek city-states had reached a watershed. The rise of the hoplite (fully-armed infantry) armies had ushered in a new type of warfare in which the manoeuvres of a well-trained body of citizen soldiers, fighting as a team, left little space for the exploits of a heroic individualist. In politics, too, the development of democracy in the fifth century BC was to limit severely the opportunities for individuals to win fame by great deeds.

Fig. 1. Athletes on a Panathenaic amphora by the Berlin Painter (early 5th century BC).

As we shall see, however, the age of tyrants gave Greek aristocrats their last chance to play the hero before the masses gained confidence in their newly-acquired votes and brushed them off the stage. These rulers were not all tyrants in the modern sense of the word but something more akin to benevolent dictators, in Athens at least. They provided a bridge of stability between aristocratic rule, often a time of struggles among leading families, and the subsequent birth-pangs of democracy.

Peisistratos and Athens

Peisistratos was the first tyrant of Athens. After two unsuccessful attempts he finally established himself as tyrant in 546 BC, where he remained until his death in 527 BC. He was succeeded by his son Hippias who went into exile as a result of Spartan intervention in 510 BC.

This was a very important period of Athenian history for two reasons. It gave respite from family feuding, and allowed the reforms of Solon to take root. Solon was an Athenian statesman who had been invited by his fellow-citizens to reform the constitution. Later, as soon as Hippias left Athens and after some months of upheaval, the first ever democracy was invented. This was made possible partly by the stability afforded by Solon's reforms, which, we are told, Peisistratos had left untouched, but also by the unprecedented expansion which had taken place in Athens. Not only had the population greatly increased but the city had become much wealthier as a result of wider trade, and Peisistratos had forged important links with overseas powers. Much of Athens' new wealth had been spent on an ambitious building programme which not only glorified the tyrants, as was intended, but also made Athens famous. This in turn encouraged the influx of more skilled and enterprising Greeks from all around. The arts flourished as never before. Black-figure vase painting reached the height of its development, red-figure vase painting was invented, and leading poets came to the tyrants' court.

By looking at these years in depth we shall begin to get the 'feel' of what it was like to live in Athens at a time of rapid expansion. It must have been like living in Florence during the early years of the Renaissance. Already, by the last quarter of the sixth century BC, Athenian art was as fine as that of any other state, her buildings were second to none, and she was about to expand her leading role in international affairs. She defeated a Persian army almost single-handed at Marathon in 490 BC, and ten years later spearheaded the Greek resistance at sea to Xerxes' invasion at the battle of Salamis. The age of Peisistratos was an essential prelude to this great drama, and the influence of Homer was part of the backcloth.

Homer and the Greek world

Peisistratos actually claimed descent from one of Homer's heroes, Nestor of Pylos, the oldest and wisest of the Greeks at Troy, a man whose epithet 'tamer of horses' no doubt influenced the names of Peisistratos' first two sons, Hippias ('The Knight') and Hipparchos ('Cavalry Commander'). We are told by the historian Herodotus (5.65) that Peisistratos himself was named after Nestor's son who became friendly with Odysseus' son Telemachos in Book 3 of the *Odyssey*. Peisistratos could have wished for no more Homeric a background than this: he had the family tree, he had the talent and the ambition, and he took his chances when they came and fully lived up to the example set by his legendary forebears.

Once established in power in Athens he is said to have introduced the annual recitation of Homer's poems, so he was himself responsible for strengthening and extending the tradition which had moulded him and his fellow-aristocrats. A century and a half later Plato, the Athenian philosopher, could say that Homer was the 'educator of Greece'.

The coming of democracy did limit the scope of would-be heroes for a while and men like Miltiades and Themistokles, who acquired considerable influence for themselves, both ended their careers in disgrace. So did Alkibiades, perhaps the most able general Athens produced in the war against Sparta at the end of the fifth century. Nevertheless, Homer's influence was to reassert itself in the Greek world in the spectacular figure of Alexander the Great of Macedon in the fourth century. This young hero who had conquered the world by the time he was thirty is said to have always carried a copy of Homer with him, and one of his first actions on reaching Asia was to visit the site of Troy. There he sacrificed to the heroes, and especially to Achilles. Perhaps Alexander was the Greek who by his Asian conquests, which were achieved through his personal courage and flair for leadership, got nearest to the condition of a Homeric hero.

Chapter 2
The Evidence

Herodotus – the Father of History

The most spectacular achievement of the year 585 BC was the prediction of a solar eclipse. Thales of Miletos, who achieved this scientific 'first', was one of the Ionian Greeks who around 600 BC began to search for logical explanations of natural phenomena. The Ionian Greeks lived in *poleis* (city-states) sprinkled down the western seaboard of Asia Minor (modern Turkey) and the nearby islands, and it was among these inquisitive intellectuals that the study of science and philosophy began.

One of their most distinguished sons was the historian Herodotus, born about 484 BC in Halikarnassos, a *polis* on a rocky peninsula north-east of the island of Kos. He applied the Ionian spirit of enquiry (the Greek word *historie* means 'enquiry' or 'research') to human affairs, and after a lifetime of asking questions published some time after 430 BC a history of the wars between the Greeks and the Persians. It is the earliest major Greek prose work to have survived intact. He states his aim in his opening sentence:

> This is an account of the enquiries of Herodotus of Halikarnassos, made so that men's achievements should not be forgotten through the passing of time, and so that great and marvellous deeds, done by both Greeks and foreigners, should win renown, and in particular the reasons why they fought against each other.
> (HERODOTUS 1.1)

Note the broad canvas: 'men's achievements...great and marvellous deeds'. Homer had sung in verse of the heroes of old. Now Herodotus commemorated in prose the new race of heroes who had created the world of the fifth century for Greeks to live in – an epic subject indeed.

The book covers far more than the campaign of Marathon in 490 BC and Xerxes' great invasion ten years later. In order to explain why East and West came into conflict, Herodotus had to go as far back as

550 BC when the Persian Empire began to expand under Cyrus the Great. The result was the first world history, a work of extraordinary range and diversity. Although he used some written sources and followed earlier writers in some of the types of information he collected, it is certain that no comparable work existed before he produced his history, and Herodotus has rightly been recognised since antiquity as the Father of History.

The work is famous for its apparent digressions, but in fact it is organised logically. For whenever Herodotus mentions a nation, tribe or *polis*, he usually sketches its earlier history, including comments on its customs, religion, political development, or whatever takes his fancy. Such an arrangement is better suited to the awkward papyrus scrolls on which it was originally written: a moment's thought shows us the frustration which would be caused by the use of footnotes or appendices. In fact his writings are much more than what we would regard as history nowadays and include anthropology, geography, ethnology, comparative religion, philology and so on.

In Book 1, after his introduction, Herodotus in a splendid sw recounts the history of Lydia – the kingdom of Croesus – which like a buffer between the Persian Empire and the Ionian Greeks. was the Persian conquest of Lydia which first confronted Greeks w Persians; and when Croesus sent to mainland Greece for help discovered that Athens and Sparta were the two most powerful stat Herodotus uses this opportunity to tell us how Peisistratos h recently seized power in Athens and what conditions were like und the tyranny (1.59- 64). Later, in Book 5, when Aristagoras the Ionia comes to Greece on a similar mission, Herodotus continues th history of Athens and describes the fall of the tyrants (5.55-65).

Herodotus used – and indeed sometimes quoted from – a number of written sources, although he was limited by knowing no language other than Greek; he also referred to what he had seen (e.g. buildings, dedications in temples, inscriptions, or monuments); but most of his information was obtained by asking questions. For the campaigns of 490 BC and 480/479 BC he was able to speak to men who had fought in the battles, but for events of the previous century he had to rely on oral tradition.

Nowadays we use oral tradition to preserve what is often parochial history – of a family, for instance, or a village, or an institution. Narrative is usually anecdotal: important events like weddings, deaths, holidays, sporting fixtures, will be recalled through incidents which are recounted with humour or nostalgia. Vivid details pinpoint a twist in the tale or illuminate an arresting character. Such stories are passed down by family, friends or colleagues. Events of wider importance, or easily forgotten minutiae, are of course committed to paper or micro-chip.

Sixth-century Greeks, on the other hand, passed on all information by word of mouth, apart from laws or constitutions which had to be remembered in precise detail and could be carved on wood or stone. (The first known book in Greek prose, written by Anaximandros of Miletos in about 550 BC, was a scientific treatise). The rich mix of Herodotus' history, which describes not only the movements of mighty armies but also intimate conversations from the Great King's bedchamber, can be attributed to the variety of the oral traditions he used as well as to his own boundless curiosity. Although his account is the only evidence for much of the narrative, rampant scepticism may be restrained by bearing in mind that the ancients, not having our easy access to libraries and data banks, had sharp memories for past events; and modern oral historians tell us that stories may be passed down several generations without serious alteration.

The important questions to ask when shaping up to an apparently dubious story in Herodotus are 'Who would have told this to him?' and 'Why would they remember this story, and how might it be altered by them?' Using such tools we can break into the treasury of his writings with some hope of finding the truth – and at the same time allow ourselves to be charmed by one of the world's greatest story-tellers.

Other sources

Other evidence for this period comes from a work discovered on papyrus only last century in Egypt entitled *The Constitution of Athens*, one of 158 constitutions said to have been collected and described by Aristotle in the fourth century BC. *The Constitution of Athens* is the only one which has survived, and it has much valuable information – though its quality is variable. It was written either by Aristotle himself, or perhaps more likely by one of his pupils. There are several chapters on Solon and the tyrants, and more than sixty lines of Solon's poetry are quoted. The author of this work will be referred to in square brackets as [Aristotle].

[Aristotle] would have read the Atthidographers, a number of local historians of Attica who began writing in the late fifth century. Their works are known to us only through quotations in other writers, and much of their information has been infected by their strong political views.

Towards the end of the fifth century the Athenian Thucydides wrote a history of the war between Athens and Sparta which broke out in 431 BC, having himself fought as a general in its early years. In his introduction he discusses the rise of tyranny in the Greek *poleis*, and in Book 6 has a lengthy digression on the murder of Peisistratos' son Hipparchos. Compared with the genial Herodotus, Thucydides is an austere writer, and his work is remarkable for its analytic qualities and intellectual rigour; yet it is clear that he cared passionately about the events he described so memorably. He states at the outset that he intended his history to be 'a possession for ever': so far, time has fully justified his claim.

Another relevant work is Plutarch's *Life of Solon*, one of fifty biographies written by a Boeotian around the end of the first century AD. Plutarch's main aim was to recreate the characters of great men so that his readers might learn from their achievements. His writings are therefore biographical rather than historical in the strictest sense; but they contain much useful information, and in his *Life of Solon* Plutarch preserves important details of Solon's reforms.

Besides these prose works, many poems and fragments of poems have survived which convey something of the flavour of this period. A number of inscriptions shed light in unexpected places, and at least a glimpse of the appearance of Athens at this time can be captured through the sculptures and pottery which adorned the city and which we can still enjoy today.

Chapter 3
Early Athens

Attica before 650 BC

Greece is a land of contrasts. If you stand on the Kithairon-Parnes range of mountains on the north-west border of Attica, looking towards Athens, Boeotia's flat and fertile plains lie behind you. In front of you the barren hills seem to roll on for ever. In fact you are at Attica's widest point, and to the south-east as it probes into the Aegean Sea the peninsula tapers to a point at Cape Sounion, some forty miles away, where Poseidon's ruined temple provides one of the most romantic sights in Greece.

Attica is about 1,000 square miles (2,500 sq. km.) in area, and in the driest part of Greece. It is rich in raw materials, silver, clay and building stone but its soil, apart from three separate plains where crops can be grown, is comparatively poor. Plato compared it to 'the skeleton of a sick man; the good soil has all been washed away, leaving the land nothing but skin and bone.' This thin soil, however, is ideal for olives, and olive trees still abound in the countryside today. In classical times they were Attica's chief export.

The Athenians themselves believed that they had lived in the city from earliest times, and there is archaeological evidence of occupation on the Acropolis going back to the Neolithic Age. The various hamlets around the city were originally independent, and Thucydides presumably echoes popular tradition when he tells how

> Theseus abolished the separate councils and governments
> of the other communities and brought them all together
> into the present city of Athens, making one council
> chamber and one seat of government for all.
> (THUCYDIDES 2.15.2)

If this was the work of one man, it must have been the culmination of a gradual process stretching over several generations. The size and variety of Attica were unusual for a Greek *polis* and this fostered rival interests among the inhabitants. Indeed, family rivalries were the main influence on Athenian politics until the end of the sixth century.

9

Detailed analysis has revealed a remarkable rise in the number of graves in Attica between 800 and 700 BC. The suggestion that this was a time of increasing wealth for the population is supported by the artistic remains, for this was when the Geometric style of pottery was created in Athens. The surge and confidence of these years are ably commemorated by the huge amphorae of the Dipylon Master which not only adorned the tombs by the road leading to the Dipylon Gate into the city from the west but were also exported as far as Cyprus and Syria. By 700 BC, or perhaps earlier, it is safe to assume that Attica was fused into a single political unity with citizenship spread throughout all its towns and villages.

There followed a century of comparative stagnation. While other *poleis* colonised all round the Mediterranean Athens absorbed her surplus population in the countryside, refraining from overseas ventures until 610 BC when she sent colonists to Sigeion and Elaious. While other *poleis* overthrew their ruling aristocracies and installed tyrannies, in Attica the traditional aristocrats who were called the Eupatridai ('men of good birth') remained comfortably in charge. Although olives were being exported, the marvellous potential of the three natural harbours at the Piraeus was yet to be exploited; and Corinth seems to have captured the foreign markets for pottery.

The stranglehold over Attica which the Eupatridai enjoyed can be partly attributed to the system of government which had developed. Previously there had been kings in Attica, like the mythical Theseus, and Athenian historians of the fourth and third centuries BC spent considerable ingenuity in concocting lists of these earlier kings, using names culled from the rich growths of legend. During the Geometric period the power of a single man had devolved upon nine *archons* (rulers) who changed every year. The king's principal functions were now shared by three men. The *basileus* (king-archon) administered many of the city's ancient rituals and retained some judicial powers, while the *polemarchos* (war leader) commanded the army. But the chief secular power lay with 'the' archon, sometimes called the *archon eponymos*, because he gave his name to the year. Thus the powers previously enjoyed by a single royal family were spread around, but they were still restricted to a comparatively limited number of aristocratic families. The other six archons were lesser officials, named *thesmothetai* (lawgivers), whose name (in Greek) suggests that they drafted and recorded the laws or judgements. Presumably they presided over less important cases.

Fig. 2. This amphora by the Dipylon Master (mid-8th century BC) is 1.55 metres tall and stood over a grave near Athens' Dipylon Gate. Its schematic figures represent a corpse lying on a bier, surrounded by male and female mourners.

All archons joined the Council of the Areiopagos after their year in office. This body, which Athenians believed had originally been set up to try cases of murder, was perhaps the descendant of the king's council. The basileus presided over it when it sat as a murder court. Its powers, based on tradition rather than law, were wide-ranging, which is hardly surprising since it comprised all the citizens with the most experience in running the state. They are described as follows in the *Constitution of Athens*:

> The Council of the Areiopagos had the task of looking after the laws, and it organised most of the city's business, and its most important affairs, having authority both to punish and to fine all offenders.
>
> (3.6)

It may even have chosen the nine archons each year, although it seems more likely that they were chosen by lot from short lists submitted by the tribes. The Council used to meet on the Areiopagos (Hill of Ares), a low hillock near the western approach to the Acropolis, where St. Paul was to preach his famous sermon to the Athenians in the first century AD (Acts of the Apostles, Chapter 17).

The rise of the tyrants

Elsewhere in Greece from around the middle of the seventh century, a new spirit was abroad. One by one the ruling aristocracies were toppled and tyrants took their place, staying in power for an average of two generations. The Greeks used the word *tyrannos* (plural *tyrannoi*) to describe them. The word does not appear in Homer and seems to be of Lydian or Phoenician origin. It had no pejorative content originally; but the behaviour of many tyrants soon gave the word the undesirable connotations which the English word 'tyrant' has. Aristotle describes them as follows:

> The tyrant is established from among the people and the mob against the nobles, so that the people may be protected from them. This is clear from the facts of history: for the great majority of tyrants have risen from being popular leaders in some sense, having won favour by their slandering of the nobles.
>
> (*Politics* 1310b)

Most had these characteristics in common: they seized power illegally; they ruled outside the law, although many ruled wisely for at least the first generation; and they were usually aristocrats themselves. Various reasons have been suggested for their appearance on the Greek scene. [Aristotle] says that the aristocratic rulers had often become unpopular. Kypselos overthrew the Bacchiadai in Corinth, who were an hereditary aristocracy, intermarrying and claiming descent from an earlier king called Bacchis. He then killed or expelled the nobles and confiscated their property.

Thucydides hints at economic reasons:

> As Greece became more powerful and as cities became even wealthier than before, tyrannies were established in nearly all the cities. The result of this was that public revenues increased, shipbuilding flourished, and men began to think of controlling the sea.
>
> (1.13)

Two forces were at work here. With the increase of trade and other ways of making money there arose a wealthy class, many of whom would be outside the governing families. Add to that a widening gap between rich and poor – for which there is evidence in Attica, so probably it was true elsewhere – and you have a brew ready to boil over at the slightest raising of the temperature. The flashpoint was reached in Megara, for instance, when Theagenes became tyrant in 640 BC after slaughtering the flocks of the wealthy.

Support for the adventurer who seized power might come from other disaffected rich men, and also from the poor. Tradition says that tyrants usually made life easier for the poor – at least in the early stages of their reigns. Other support might come from the developing hoplite armies, citizens who could afford to buy their own armour and now had no need in battle for the protection of the aristocracy in the brave new world of team-fighting which had replaced the old world of single combat.

Some at least of these conditions which produced tyranny elsewere can be seen in Athens towards the end of the seventh century BC. Yet it was nearly a hundred years before the first Athenian tyrant seized power. One reason may well have been that by sharing the former king's power among nine archons the Eupatridai dissipated the head of steam which would have built up if this power had been restricted to a single family, as it was in Corinth.

Kylon and Dracon

A certain Kylon had won the middle-distance race in the Olympics in
640 BC. He was a Eupatrid and had married the daughter of
Theagenes, tyrant of Megara. Inspired perhaps by first-hand
experience of life in a tyrant's court, when visiting his in-laws, he
'preened himself with thoughts of becoming tyrant' (Herodotus 5.71).
When consulted, the oracle at Delphi advised him to seize the
Acropolis on the day of the greatest festival of Zeus – a good time
for a coup d'etat when the men would be otherwised engaged.
Thucydides suggests (as Delphi doubtless did after the event) that the
Diasia, an Athenian festival to Zeus held outside the city, was
intended. But Kylon chose the Olympics 'considering them
appropriate,' Thucydides adds drily, 'in view of his own Olympic
victory' (1.126.5).

With friends of his own and help from his father-in-law Kylon
captured the Acropolis (c. 630 BC); but instead of joining him, as he
must have hoped, the army besieged him there, commanded by other
aristocrats. He and his brother escaped, but his supporters were
eventually killed by the Athenians. The precise details of what
happened are unclear. Athenians later believed that these deaths, in
a holy place, had brought down a curse on the city, and the noble
family of the Alkmeonidai were blamed, one of whom, Megakles, was
archon at the time. In later years this family was twice expelled from
Athens on the pretext of causing the sacrilege. The facts of what
happened must have been argued over many times, and this would
account for the contradictions in the sources.

Whether Theagenes was the driving force behind the attempted
coup, or whether Kylon was a disinterested champion of the people
or a frustrated noble with delusions of grandeur, we cannot tell. What
is clear is that Athenians were not prepared to support a tyrant. They
may also have resented Megarian interference. Attention should be
drawn at this point to the first appearance of the Alkmeonidai upon
the Athenian stage. They were to play an important part in years to
come.

In 621-620 BC the first written Athenian code of laws was drawn
up by Dracon. This was presumably one result of Kylon's failed
conspiracy and may be seen as an attempt by the aristocracy to share
their power more fairly with each other. It was at the same time an
enlightened move. Written laws, with fixed penalties, are open to
criticism and alteration, and at his trial the accused is less exposed to

the whim of an upper-class judge.

Dracon's laws acquired a reputation for severity (they have given us the modern word 'Draconian'), and Aristotle commented that 'they contained nothing remarkable except the harshness of the penalties.' (*Politics* 1274b16). These included the death penalty for attempted tyranny, as well as for lesser crimes like theft. Other offences were punished by fines measured in numbers of oxen.

Many cities produced codes of laws during the seventh century and often these lasted for a long time. In Athens, however, Dracon's code was not successful in easing the tension between rich and poor. Only his law on murder survived, and was still in use in the fourth century. The others were all swept away by Solon a generation later.

Chapter 4
Solon

Solon and the crisis in Attica

> I know, and grief lies deep in my heart,
> When I behold the oldest land of Ionia ablaze.
>
> (SOLON frag.4a)

Kylon and Dracon are shadowy figures, but Solon bursts into Athenian history with a freshness and immediacy unique in the sixth century. You would search far to find a politician of such stature who wrote poetry to present his programme for reform, and justify it afterwards. But Solon did just that. He is said to have written over five thousand lines of verse, and enough of it (almost 300 lines) has survived for us to see him in sharp focus as poet, politician and sage, after the haze of the preceding centuries. [Aristotle] describes him as 'a leading citizen in birth and reputation, but one of the moderates in wealth and position' (*Constitution of Athens*, 5.3), and in 594/3 BC he was appointed mediator and archon.

But what was the crisis he described in the lines on Athens quoted above? Unfortunately, Solon himself refers to it in metaphorical terms, and even his actual reforms are never described in detail – he would not wish to divulge them before the proper time, and after the event his readers would be familiar with them. Nevertheless, we can deduce a certain amount from his poems. Clearly the situation was tense; as he wrote afterwards,

> I turned at bay like a wolf among a pack of hounds.
>
> (SOLON 36.27)

[Aristotle] describes the crisis as follows:

> For a long time there was strife (*stasis*) between the notables [i.e. prominent, well-known people] and the masses. For the Athenian constitution was in all other respects an oligarchy [rule by the few], and in particular the poor were enslaved to the rich – themselves, their children and their wives...The whole land belonged to a few men. The hardest and bitterest aspect of their life as citizens was

16

the fact that they were slaves. Not that they did not have other complaints as well, for they had, so to speak, no share in anything at all.

> *(Constitution of Athens 2)*

According to [Aristotle], who presumably had access to all the poems, Solon 'always put all the blame for the civil strife on the rich,' and he quotes from another poem:

> But calm the bold spirit in your hearts,
> You who have grabbed too many good things;
> Restrain your thrusting ambition.

> *(Constitution of Athens 5.3)*

Several reasons for civil strife elsewhere have already been discussed. Overpopulation had driven other states to found colonies a century earlier at a time when Athenians were colonising Attica itself, and it seems not to have been a problem in Attica, even at this stage. The greed of the rich and the debts incurred by everyone else seem to be at the root of the crisis. Perhaps it only took two or three poor harvests to bankrupt the small landowners who were forced to mortgage their land, and incur debts they could never repay. Such debt must have been a major problem in Attica, judging by what Solon wrote after his reforms; although allowance should perhaps be made for the political reformer's justification of what he has done. It is not clear just what 'slavery' means in line 7:

> I brought back to Athens, to their home which the gods established,
> Many men who had been sold, some unjustly,
> Some justly, and some forced to flee because of debt
> Who were no longer speaking Attic,
> As they had been wandering in many places.
> Others, who were suffering shameful slavery right here,
> Trembling at their masters' moods, I set free.

> (SOLON 36.8-15)

'Slavery' must at least have meant that the rich in some way interfered with the freedom of action of the 'slaves', and the resentment this caused was steadily building up. The publication of Dracon's laws would have brought into the open the all too firm grip which the Eupatridai enjoyed over the people, and there must have been constant discussion of these laws – and pressure to change them. Most effective pressure may well have come from a new hoplite class, the existence of which is suggested by evidence from other *poleis*.

These men would now be aware of their inferior status, spelled out in Dracon's code, and eager to assert themselves in the face of Eupatrid domination, and even the threats to their freedom implicit in the fate of those who had been 'enslaved'.

Solon's reforms

Solon's approach to this mixture of economic, social and political problems was decisive and far-reaching. In [Aristotle's] words,

> When he gained control of affairs, Solon set the people free, both for the present and for the future, by forbidding loans on the security of the person; he also passed laws, and caused a cancellation of debts, both private and public, which the Athenians call the 'Shaking off of Burdens', since they have shaken off the weight which oppressed them.
>
> (*Constitution of Athens* 6.1)

This *seisachtheia* (shaking off of burdens) must surely be a vivid metaphor coined by Solon himself; and he applied his 'slavery' imagery to the land as well as to its inhabitants when he wrote about freeing 'the Earth which was once enslaved' (36.7).

In their search for the precise details of Solon's economic reforms, modern writers are hampered by the absence of specific ancient evidence. Even [Aristotle], writing about 250 years later, clearly found himself wrestling with concepts which were already obsolete. Any modern theory which explains what Solon did, and why, involves a certain degree of speculation. Indeed, the true explanation would require knowledge of a system of land tenure, and its resultant obligations between classes, which was lost and forgotten even by [Aristotle]'s time. Following Solon, he described the rapacity of the rich as the fundamental problem. Their greed, combined with the new aspirations of many landowners, and the effect of both these factors on the poorer citizens, had led to an impasse which could only be solved by civil war – or, to Athens' good fortune, by the appearance of an arbitrator like Solon who was respected by both sides in the dispute. At any rate he got rid of the worst abuses, and future confrontations arose for reasons other than debt.

> I wrote down laws for the bad and good alike,
> Applying honest justice to each man.
>
> (SOLON 36.18-20)

In his political reforms, too, Solon followed the principle of justice. From now on, wealth rather than birth was to be the basis of political power – a fundamental change for the men of Athens. Solon divided the citizens into four classes. The first class, the *pentakosiomedimnoi*, consisted of those whose land produced 500 measures or more of corn or wine. The name means '500 medimnoi' and the medimnos was a substantial measure (It is often translated as 'bushel' in English; one bushel equals 36 liquid litres). Only members of this class could hold the archonship or become state treasurers. Minor offices were distributed (we do not know how) between the next two classes: the *hippeis* ('cavalrymen'), whose land produced 300 medimnoi or more, and the *zeugitai* ('men of the yoke', probably meaning men who fought in close formation together, i.e. hoplites), whose land produced 200-300 medimnoi. The lowest class, the *thetes* ('labourers'), were those with less than 200 medimnoi, and they had access only to the assembly and the lawcourt. It was possible, however, to move from one class to another. [Aristotle] refers to a statue of a man and a horse on the Acropolis with this inscription:

> Anthemion son of Diphilos made this dedication to the gods when he rose from the labourers' class to be a cavalryman.
>
> *(Constitution of Athens 7.4)*

Continuing his description of Solon's reforms, [Aristotle] writes:

> Solon had the office-holders appointed by lot from short lists chosen by each of the tribes. Each tribe chose ten candidates for the nine archonships, and lots were drawn among these.
>
> *(Constitution of Athens 8.1)*

The opening of the archonship to wealthy men outside the charmed circle of the Eupatridai must have caused considerable high blue blood pressure. This would have been eased by leaving the final choice to the gods rather than men, which was how the Greeks viewed the use of the lot. As all ex-archons became members of the Council of the Areiopagos for life, its membership would, as time passed, become more representative of the wealthier, non-aristocratic end of Athenian society.

Another radical move by Solon was the establishment of a Council of 400, 100 from each tribe – the forerunner of the later Council of 500 instituted by the reformer Kleisthenes in 508 BC, and one of the pillars of Athenian democracy. Plutarch is perhaps echoing another of Solon's own metaphors when he says:

His intention was that, with its two Councils, the state should ride at double anchor, so to speak, and so be more sheltered from the buffetings of party politics and better able to provide tranquillity for the people.

(Life of Solon 19.2)

The functions of this body are not known for certain. Plutarch (19.1) says it was a probouleutic body, meaning that it prepared business for the Assembly, drew up the agenda and so on.

An inscription of the first half of the sixth century BC gives us a fascinating glimpse of the constitution of Chios, an island just off the Ionian coast, a little more than half the size of Attica. The best-preserved part reads:

...if he has been wronged in the court of the *demarchos* (officer of the people) [let him deposit x] staters, and let him appeal to the council of the people. On the ninth day of every month the council of the people is to assemble under penalty*, elected, fifty from each tribe. Let it carry out the other affairs of the people and also all the judgements which have been appealed against during the past month, [let it?]

(Greek Historical Inscriptions, no.8)

Unfortunately the final main verb is missing, and we do not know whether the council was to judge these appeals itself or simply prepare them for inclusion in the business of the assembly. Nevertheless, there is evidence here for a people's council on Chios carrying out public business, and somehow involved in a right of appeal against decisions of the magistrates.

Was the same wind of change blowing through both Chios and Athens in the early years of the sixth century? Many scholars think so and, if this is true, then Solon's Council of 400 was a vital instrument in weakening Eupatrid control over the lawcourts. In addition, the formation of this body, as well as limiting the powers of the Areiopagos, suggests a more significant role for the Assembly of all the citizens. Did it perhaps meet more regularly now? We do not know; but [Aristotle] says that Solon gave the people the right of appeal to 'the jury court', an anachronistic term which some believe

---

*This could mean either 'with power to exact penalties', or 'under penalty for non-attendance'.

refers to the full assembly. It may refer to the Council of 500. At any rate [Aristotle] was not exaggerating when he wrote 'men say that this more than anything else gave power to the people' (*Constitution of Athens*, 9.1), although it is only fair to add that this power did not become a reality until the introduction of pay for juries in the 460s BC.

It is tempting to see in all these arrangements a prototype of the democracy which was to be established later. But almost ninety years were still to pass. The aristocrats did not relinquish power to the people so easily, and the people remained dissatisfied.

> Solon opposed both parties; and although he could have joined either side and become tyrant, he chose to incur the hatred of both sides by saving his country and passing the best laws he could.
>
> *(Constitution of Athens* 11.2)

[Aristotle] ends his account of Solon's reforms by quoting another poem. 'If another man had been given this position of authority,' he writes,

> He would not have held the people back, nor restrained them,
> Until he had stirred up the milk and taken away the cream.
> But I stood in no man's land, as it were,
> Like a marker.
>
> (SOLON 37.7-10)

In fact Solon laid down several markers which, we can see with hindsight, pointed the way to Kleisthenes' democracy at the end of the century; and his great contribution to Athenian history was the establishment of fairness as the basis of social relations, and wealth rather than birth as the key to political power.

Although some of his political settlement was short-lived, and proved to be premature for archaic Athens, it is interesting to see that the ancient world did not fail to appreciate him as a wise man, and he was soon enrolled as one of the Seven Sages of antiquity. Herodotus devotes four pages to Solon's philosophical conversations with King Croesus of Lydia, and four lines to his laws. It is unlikely that they ever met – the story is probably apocryphal – but there is a certain poignancy in the advice Solon gave to Croesus, to 'call no man happy until he is dead'. Croesus, the story goes, remembered these words when sitting on a pyre awaiting death after his kingdom had been conquered by the Persians. (Herodotus 1.29-33 and 86). Did Solon himself ruefully remember his advice when, shortly before his own death, his distant relative Peisistratos seized the Acropolis in his first attempt to become tyrant of Athens?

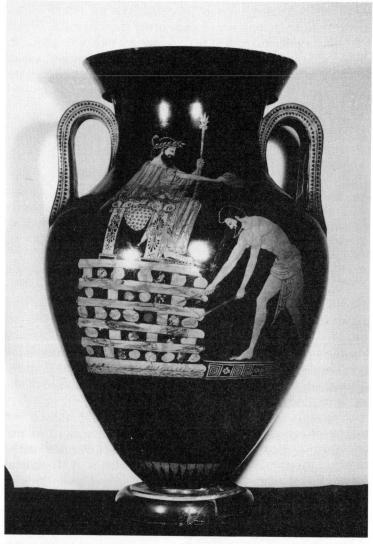

Fig. 3. Croesus on the pyre, from an Athenian red-figure belly amphora by Myson (early 5th century BC). A rare example of an illustration of a historical figure, if not of a historical event.

Chapter 5
Third Time Lucky

From Solon to Peisistratos

Solon went on a world tour for ten years, leaving the Athenians to sort themselves out.

> While Solon was away, there was still confusion in the city, but peace reigned for four years. In the fourth year after Solon's rule, however, no archon was elected owing to the civil strife (*stasis*), and again, four years later, the same thing happened. After another four-year gap, Damasias was elected archon and held office for two years and two months until he was removed by force. The Athenians then decided to appoint ten archons on account of the *stasis*... and they held power for the year after Damasias.
>
> (*Constitution of Athens* 13)

After the bright light shed by the sources on 594 BC, comparative gloom shrouds the next thirty years of Athenian history. That the first decade should be bedevilled by conflict over the election of archons is hardly surprising seeing that Solon had opened up the highest office to non-Eupatrid families. Kylon had been the first to attempt a tyranny (see ch. 3 above). Now Damasias tried, but without any lasting success. After this, little is known of political developments, but there are nevertheless enough glimmers for us to be able to construct a shadowy outline of economic developments during these years before the appearance of Peisistratos.

Some aspects of Solon's legislation help us to pierce the darkness. Plutarch says that oil was the only local product which Solon allowed the Athenians to export (*Life of Solon* 24.1). This law has been interpreted in various ways. It may well have been intended to force the wealthy to stop exporting their surplus grain abroad, thus freeing it for internal use. It would also have increased olive production, although this would be a gradual process, as an olive tree takes twenty years to reach maturity.

Plutarch also tells us that under Solon's laws a son was not compelled to support his father unless he had been taught a trade by him (22.1). In addition, immigrants were only allowed to become Athenian citizens if they were permanent exiles from their own countries, or came with their whole families to practise a trade (24.4). Such measures would clearly encourage craft-industry groups; and the latter two groups must have been in part responsible for the arrival in Athens of Corinthian potters, seen in the changing Athenian styles in the early part of the century, and for the remarkable increase in the export of Athenian pottery at this time.

The Agora, the public area to the north-west of the Acropolis, had been used as a gathering-place from soon after 700 BC, and the earliest surviving buildings date from the beginning of the sixth century BC. Traces have been found of what looks like a public building beneath the remains of the fifth-century Council-House. Could this have been used by Solon's Council of 400? The construction of such a building suggests a new confidence in post-Solonian Athens.

Other archaeological evidence which affords a glimpse into these years is the series of male and female marble statues which begins early in the century. The Attic statues which can reasonably be dated to the years 600 to 570 comprise over a third of all surviving Greek statues from that period. Some were dedicated in sanctuaries, others were erected over graves; their quality is superb. Are they evidence that the wealthy citizens of Athens, now enjoying or competing for real political power for the first time, were flexing their social muscles by commissioning such expensive works of art?

For years, Athens and Megara had been fighting over the island of Salamis, which lies to the west of Phaleron where the Athenians beached their ships at this time. Indeed Plutarch tells an anecdote about Solon going into the Agora and reciting one of his poems (fragments of which survive) in order to shame the Athenians into renewing their efforts to recapture Salamis. It is not clear when these efforts were successful; but Peisistratos came to fame when, probably as *polemarchos*, he led an Athenian expedition which captured Nisaea, the port of Megara. Some time before 560 BC Athens seems to have gained a measure of control over Salamis in an attempt to ensure safe passage in and out of her own harbour.

Underpinning all this new activity was Solon's code of laws, which we know from surviving fragments to have been detailed and far-reaching. They helped to emphasise the spirit of fairness and equal opportunity which was now spreading among the wealthier

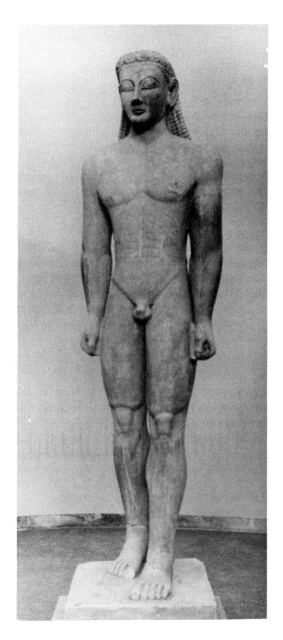

Fig. 4. Kouros from Sounion (3.05 metres high), about 590-580 BC.

inhabitants of Athens. Solon's policy of drawing in and encouraging all the available talent in Attica was paying off. It is sometimes said that Solon failed, and he certainly failed to put an end to *stasis* and the ruinous ambitions of the artistocracy. On the other hand, the steadily increasing prosperity of Attica during these years can only be seen as success. Athens was now waking from the slumber of the seventh century, stirred by Solon's far-sighted and revolutionary reforms.

Peisistratos and the three groups

Peisistratos steps into history against a background of warring factions in Attica.

> While there was strife between the men of the coast, under the command of Megakles the son of Alkmeon, and the men from the plain, under Lykourgos the son of Aristolaides, Peisistratos, with tyranny in mind, organised a third party, collecting supporters and taking command of the men from beyond the hills, as they were called.
>
> (HERODOTUS 1.59.3)

[Aristotle] gives each group a political manifesto, claiming that Megakles' party aimed for 'the middle type of constitution', Lykourgos' for 'oligarchy' (this is a Greek word which means 'rule by a few'), while Peisistratos 'seemed to favour the people most' (*Constitution of Athens* 13.4). Although this smacks of the fourth century political theorist, there is nevertheless a certain plausibility about these neatly contrasting parties and policies.

If the men from the plain lived in the great plain north-east of Athens, they were most likely predominantly Eupatridai who would originally have owned this fertile land. It is hardly surprising that they looked back with nostalgia, as long-established grandees will, to the golden age before Solon when they called the tune throughout Attica. They may even have dreamed of a reversal of Solon's reforms.

It is not clear whether the men from the coast belonged only to the area around Cape Sounion, or to the whole coast of Attica; but the estates of the Alkmeonidai, Megakles' family, are believed to have been in the area around Anaphlystos – towards the south-eastern tip of the promontory. It is arguable that the non-Eupatrids, many perhaps traders who had recently acquired their wealth, would live in the less fertile land away from the plains. But there is no evidence for this. At any rate those who wished to preserve the status quo (a 'middle type of constitution') would be those who had gained most from Solon's reforms, namely the wealthy but less aristocratic families. Whatever the policies of the men from the coast, we shall see that Megakles made alliances with both sides during the intrigues of the next few years. However, this may tell us more about the adaptability of his opportunistic family than about his political aims.

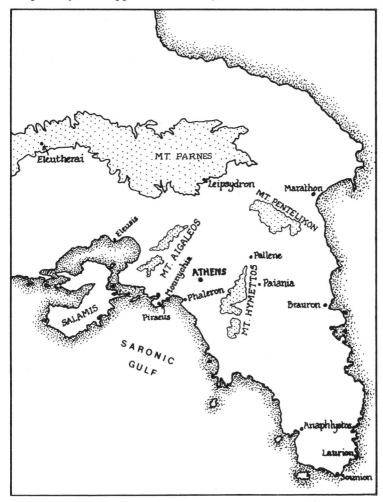

Fig. 5. Map of Attica.

It is difficult to pin down precisely the source of Peisistratos' supporters. The Greek words used to describe them could mean either 'men from beyond the hills' or, more likely, 'Hill-men', and it seems that they came from an area stretching from Mount Parnes to Brauron in north-east Attica. Peisistratos' own estates were at Brauron, (distinguished today by the lovely ruins of a sanctuary of Artemis). Much of this area could certainly be described as hill-country; presumably the inhabitants would be poorer, and it was far enough from the city for them to feel cut off from the political action. Yet these are scarcely sufficient causes to bind together and galvanise an effective third party, and in fact they were not.

[Aristotle] adds two more groups which joined Peisistratos' party:

> ...those who suffered hardship because they had been deprived of the debts they were owed, and those who were afraid because they were not of pure Athenian descent.
>
> (*Constitution of Athens* 13.5)

The former of these seems to refer to nobles who were impoverished by Solon's cancellation of debts, and had still not recovered a generation later – not, surely, a significant number. The latter group, for whose existence [Aristotle] adduces evidence dating from after the tyranny, has yet to be satisfactorily explained.

It is hard to escape the conclusion that we are in danger here of letting the waters be muddied by the rationalisations of later theorists. The obvious answer is that each party took its political programme, or bias, primarily from its leader, and that geographical or socio-economic factors played a far less important part. Herodotus has often been criticised for seeing only individuals as responsible for great events in his history, and not the popular movements beloved of later historians; but here he may have hit the nail on the head. If analysing Peisistratos' programme and party is problematic, then we should perhaps after all pay more attention to Herodotus, our earliest source, when he says that Peisistratos 'organised a third party' and took 'command of the men from beyond the hills' (1.59.3). In other words, he found supporters where he could, made alliances when and where he could, and, as we shall see, only succeeded in the end by using mercenaries and foreign cash. If he did champion the poor, they were too few or weak to add a decisive impetus to his ambitions. He was at first only one of several nobles vying for power , and he owed his final success to his foreign connections, his military skill and his flair for public relations.

If at first you don't succeed...

Into this confused situation the purposeful Peisistratos made a dramatic entry – in his chariot at full speed, and covered in blood. Let Herodotus tell the story:

> He devised the following plan: after wounding himself and his mules he drove his chariot into the Agora as if he had just escaped from his enemies, who had intended to murder him, presumably, while he was driving into the country. Then he asked the people to give him a bodyguard, for he had previously distinguished himself in the war against Megara in which, as the Athenian commander, he had captured Nisaea and performed other notable deeds. The Athenian people were taken in and enlisted a number of citizens for him who followed him as a bodyguard, carrying clubs rather than spears. These men, led by Peisistratos, rose up together and captured the Acropolis.
>
> (1.59.4)

Peisistratos was now about forty years old. We know nothing of his earlier life except for his capture of the Megarian port of Nisaea, which left him on the crest of a wave of popular acclaim. Herodotus implies that this was why the people agreed to give him a bodyguard. This victory had been a major step towards gaining control of Salamis, which the Athenians had recently achieved after years of bickering and fighting with Megara.

Both Herodotus and [Aristotle] say his wounds were self-inflicted: this is quite possible, judging by what we know of his instinct for propaganda. But it should be remembered, of course, that his enemies would never have admitted to ambushing him – especially when they failed to do the job properly. If he did survive an assassination attempt, then it can only be said that he showed a singular knack for catching that 'tide in the affairs of men, which, taken at the flood, leads on to fortune.'

Peisistratos must have been aware that he had the ability to impose some sort of order on Athens, given the opportunity, but the best he could hope for under Solon's constitution was a year as archon. His war service had proved his courage and administrative powers. Perhaps asking for a bodyguard, or getting a friend to do so (his name was Aristion, according to [Aristotle]), was the crucial test of his popularity. He passed it, and events were to prove that his self-confidence was well-founded.

As Herodotus continues:

> Then Peisistratos ruled over the Athenians, without disturbing the existing magistracies or changing the laws. He governed the city in an orderly and wise fashion, in accordance with the established customs.
>
> (1.59.6)

However, the tide did not run smoothly straight away:

> Not long after, the parties of Megakles and Lykourgos joined forces and drove him out. This was how Peisistratos first got control of Athens and, before his tyranny had properly taken root, lost it again. But fighting broke out afresh among those who had expelled him.
>
> Megakles was getting the worse of the fight, so he suggested to Peisistratos that he would help him to become tyrant again if he agreed to marry his daughter. Peisistratos agreed to the terms Megakles proposed, and together they devised for his return by far the most ridiculous charade I have ever heard of. From ancient times Greeks have been considered more clever and free from silliness than other nations, and yet it was among the Athenians, who were said to be the cleverest of the Greeks, that these two contrived the following nonsense.
>
> In the village of Paiania there was a woman called Phye, who was almost six feet tall, and generally good-looking. They dressed her in full armour, mounted her on a chariot, showed her how to pose in the most striking way, and drove her to the city. They had sent some heralds ahead, who arrived in the city and made the following proclamation, as they had been instructed:
>
> 'O men of Athens, receive Peisistratos with a good will! Athene herself has honoured him above other men and is escorting him to her own Acropolis!' When they had gone round announcing this, the news quickly reached the villages as well that Athene was bringing Peisistratos back, and in the city, believing that the woman was the goddess herself, they worshipped her and welcomed Peisistratos.
>
> (HERODOTUS 1.60.2-5)

This delightful anecdote has several interesting facets: First there is the glimpse of Herodotus the Ionian intellectual, complimenting the Athenians on their quick-wittedness one moment, and appearing scandalised by their gullibility the next. But his scepticism is a century too early: he attributes to the Athenians a sophistication their descendants may have developed by his own time, but which can scarcely have existed in Attica a hundred years earlier. Many citizens probably did believe there was something supernatural about the whole business, and those who saw through the charade would no doubt cheerfully go along with it for what it was – a carefully organised declaration of who was now in charge, with religious overtones. At any rate they had little choice, and perhaps many did not care.

Some critics believe that this is a tall story in more ways than one, but Phye's ride (her name means 'stature') was not meant to explain why or how Peisistratos got back into power. The deal had been fixed by the two families behind the scenes – Phye was merely the icing on the cake: this was a lap of honour with Athene on board. Tableaux on floats are still the stuff of local pageants.

So we see here Peisistratos beginning to develop his sure touch for public relations. For him this was a preliminary canter in the propaganda stakes. By the time he was properly installed as tyrant, and in mid-season form, we shall find him indulging in wholesale manipulation of religion by creating state festivals.

Even so his best-laid schemes failed to prosper despite, or rather because of, the help of Megakles and the Alkmeonidai.

> After regaining the tyranny in this way, Peisistratos married Megakles' daughter, in accordance with their agreement. But because he had grown-up sons of his own, and the Alkmeonidai were said to be under a curse, he did not want to have children by his new wife and so did not sleep with her in the usual way. At first his wife kept this secret, but eventually, whether in answer to a question or not, she told her mother, who told Megakles. He was so angry at being insulted by Peisistratos that he made peace with his political enemies, and when Peisistratos learned of the plot against him he left the country altogether and went to Eretria, where he discussed the situation with his sons.
>
> (1.61.1-2)

Herodotus shows considerable human insight in this extract. Peisistratos, ambitious for his own family and mistrusting the shifty Alkmeonidai, is unwilling to pollute the pure Peisistratid blood and endanger his own sons' inheritance (did his son Hippias put his oar in even at this stage?); the luckless unnamed wife, a pawn in the dynastic struggles of Athens during these turbulent years, at last, as girls will, tells all to her mother (who was no doubt equally anxious about the succession, as Herodotus suggests); and Megakles himself, perhaps sorry that he had given pride of place to Peisistratos, albeit the better man, and furious when he discovers his family is not going to share it in the next generation, is now willing even to ditch their agreement to save the family name – all this rings true, and is deftly sketched by the historian. It is also compelling evidence of the level at which these intrigues were pursued: at the tables, and in the beds, of the leading families.

His final sentence suggests that Peisistratos remained in Attica after losing power the first time, but that now it was not safe to remain. Or perhaps he even decided to give up. The next extract implies that Hippias, with an eye no doubt to his own future, provided the initial impetus for the third and final attempt.

Tyrant at last

Hippias persuaded them that they should take over the tyranny again, so they began to collect contributions from cities which were under any sort of obligation to them. They collected large sums of money from many sources, but the Thebans were by far the most generous. Time passed and, to cut a long story short, everything was eventually ready for their return. Argive mercenaries joined them from the Peloponnese, and a man called Lygdamis came as a volunteer from Naxos, providing not only his enthusiastic support but also money and men. Over ten years had passed when they set off from Eretria and returned to Attica.

The first place they captured was Marathon. When they were encamped here, their supporters from the city joined them and others flowed in from the villages who preferred tyranny to freedom. These forces pitched camp together, but the Athenians in the city paid no attention while Peisistratos was gathering support, nor again when he occupied Marathon. However, when they heard that he was marching from Marathon to the city, they set out to meet the invaders with their whole army. Meanwhile Peisistratos and his followers, setting out from Marathon to attack the city, arrived at the temple of Athene at Pallene, where they took up their position intending to join battle. Amphilytos, the soothsayer from Akarnania, following divine guidance, came up to Peisistratos and made for him the following prophecy in hexameter verse:

> 'Cast is the net, the meshes spread out wide,
> In rush the tunnies in the bright moonlight.'

Peisistratos understood these inspired words, said he accepted the oracle, and led his army forward.

The Athenians from the city were having their midday meal at the time, and some of them were playing dice after the meal, or enjoying a siesta; and so Peisistratos and his army fell on the Athenians and routed them. As they fled, Peisistratos thought of a very clever plan to prevent the Athenians from getting together again, and to keep them split up. He sent his sons out on horseback and told them, whenever they overtook any fugitives, to encourage them not to have any fears but to go back to their own homes.

The Athenians obeyed, and so for the third time Peisistratos gained control of Athens.

(HERODOTUS 1.61.3 – 64.1)

In fact there was nothing lucky about the beginning of Peisistratos' third tyranny. He had used various combinations of force and guile in his two previous attempts. This time he used sufficient force, with a touch of guile where it was needed, at the battle of Pallene.

Eretria was a natural base for his preparations. Athenians living on or near Attica's eastern coast (as Peisistratos did) had long enjoyed close links with Euboea, the rugged island which lay 'like a scabbard along the flank of Central Greece'. In his attempts to keep his Peisistratos digression reasonably concise, Herodotus makes his ten years of preparation sound like a brisk whip round any friendly cities (61.3). [Aristotle] provides more detail:

> First he settled in a place called Rhaikelos in the Thermaic Gulf; then he went on to the region around Mount Pangaion, where he obtained money and hired soldiers; then he went to Eretria.
>
> (*Constitution of Athens* 15.2)

We know so little about Peisistratos before 561 BC that we can only guess at how or when he developed such widespread contacts. Rhaikelos seems to have been an Eretrian colony, perhaps founded at this time opposite Methone in the Gulf of Therme; and Herodotus later mentions the River Strymon (64.1), near Mount Pangaion, as a source of revenue. The area was famous for its gold and silver mines, which would be an obvious motive for establishing an interest there. Peisistratos' second wife, Timonassa, whom he married some time before Megakles' daughter, was the daughter of an Argive named Gorgilos: this explains the mercenaries from Argos. She had previously been married to one of the Kypselid family who were tyrants in Corinth. Peisistratos' first (Athenian) wife, the mother of Hippias and Hipparchos, must have died or been divorced earlier. Lygdamis seems to have been a personal friend who agreed to help, and Peisistratos returned the favour soon afterwards by helping to instal him as tyrant of Naxos. These various connections, then, at least make sense even if the details are vague.

Thebes, on the other hand, is the big surprise. It is simply not known why the city which was to be at loggerheads with Athens for so many years (thanks to the skilful diplomacy of King Kleomenes of Sparta later in the century), should have been so conspicuously generous to the future tyrant of Athens.

The thoroughness of Peisistratos' preparations is impressive. With strong support from his sons he spent his ten years well, collecting help in considerable quantity from a wide area. He must have been a persuasive man: an exile from Attica who had already failed twice was hardly a good prospect for potential backers; but the few anecdotes which survive about him stress his friendliness and personal charm – what we would nowadays call charisma (itself a Greek word meaning 'grace' or 'favour').

Solon (Frag.23) wrote that one requisite of happiness for the man of means was the possession of 'a friend in foreign parts.' Peisistratos certainly proved this true, and his behaviour at this time, and later too, is another reminder of the Homeric tradition in which he moved. One of the most attractive threads running through the *Iliad* and the *Odyssey* is the concept of *xenia*. There is no English equivalent of this word, usually translated as 'guest-friendship'. When on his travels one upper-class Greek visited another – and this would happen regularly in the absence of anything like our modern hotels – they would exchange gifts and from then on be 'guest-friends', a relationship which existed for their mutual benefit, and could extend to the next generation. We can only assume that Peisistratos had been diligently collecting guest-friends during his earlier life, and that many of them were willing to help him when the call came.

Meanwhile, back in Athens, nothing is known about the

aristocratic in-fighting which presumably had been continuing for ten years. Perhaps there had been enough disruption of normal life for many Athenians to be glad to see Peisistratos return and take a firm line. His previous departures had been forced on him by other nobles and not by any popular uprising against him; and Herodotus' remarks about the orderly and traditional rule during his first tyranny suggest that he had been liked well enough by the people in general. At any rate a number of them joined him when he sailed over from Eretria. But he was taking no chances this time: he arrived with enough mercenaries to settle the issue once and for all.

Given his base on Euboea, Marathon was the obvious landing-place, the shore which was to become famous for a much more dangerous invasion over fifty years later. It was also near Peisistratos' home ground, and the support duly flowed in, from the city as well as the country villages. Herodotus' remark about those who 'preferred tyranny to freedom' may be an anachronistic comment by the fifth century historian, or a strand in the narrative which derives from a source hostile to the tyranny.

Pallene, on the main road from Marathon to Athens, is in the pass between Mount Pentelikos and the north end of Mount Hymettos, only about seven miles from the city. The slow response in Athens to his arrival may have been due to lack of unified or decisive leadership. At any rate the ensuing battle – thanks to Peisistratos' clever tactics – seems to have been almost a formality. Did he leak the contents of the oracle, and then consciously reverse its apparent reference to an enveloping movement by night? He could always claim, putting a devout face on it, that a moonlit night was the oracle's ambiguous way of describing broad daylight. The religious touch is typical of both Peisistratos and Herodotus.

[Aristotle] rounds off his account of these events with a neat anecdote about how Peisistratos held an assembly, spoke too softly to be heard, and when the people had gathered closer to him had his men confiscate their arms.

> …when he had finished the rest of his speech, he told them what had happened to their arms and ordered them not to be surprised or dismayed, but to go away and look after their private affairs: he would take care of all public affairs.
> (*Constitution of Athens* 15.5)

It would be pleasant to believe this story, but it is dangerously similar to one told by Thucydides about Hippias in 514 BC. Besides, if Herodotus had heard it told of Peisistratos, he would hardly have resisted including it in his version.

So, whether he disarmed the Athenians literally or only metaphorically, Peisistratos, like Odysseus, had returned home at last and defeated his enemies. By now he was in his middle fifties: he had waited a long time. Winston Churchill built a famous wall on his estate during his wilderness years; Peisistratos built a complex web of alliances and relationships which paid handsome dividends in 546 BC.

Herodotus' account suggests that Peisistratos had thought of throwing in the towel and retiring from tyranny after his second failure. It is ironic to think that we may have Hippias to thank for the enlightened rule of Peisistratos – the same Hippias who by ruling more harshly after his father and brother had died was driven out in 510 BC, thus bringing tyranny in Athens to an end.

Chapter 6
The Rivals

Keeping order

Although Peisistratos was now the undisputed ruler of Athens, staying in power was not necessarily going to be easy. Judging by his two failures and the fact that he had needed foreign mercenaries to carry him to victory, there were plenty of rivals who would eagerly seize any chance to topple him from his position. Besides, he did not have to look far to see how ephemeral tyrannies could be; indeed, few lasted beyond the second generation. Solon had written 'It is easy to raise a tyrant up – not to pull him down', but he was wrong. In Peisistratos' own lifetime the fate of the Kypselids of Corinth and the Orthagorids of Sikyon provided a Damoclean sword to remind him of how precarious his power was.

To neutralise this threat he took firm action. Some of his fellow-aristocrats had been killed at Pallene.

> He took as hostages the children of those Athenians who had remained behind and not fled immediately, and put them on the island of Naxos which he had conquered and handed over to Lygdamis.
>
> (HERODOTUS 1.64.1)

On the other hand, he provided continuity for the people in general, and a share of the power for nobles who toed the line. Thucydides tells us that

> ...the city was governed by the existing laws, except that the tyrants always took care to have one of their own number as one of the magistrates.
>
> (THUCYDIDES 6.54.6)

[Aristotle] sums up the reign as follows:

> Many of the nobility and of the common people supported him; he won over the former by diplomacy, and the latter by his help in their private affairs, and his behaviour towards both classes was honourable.
>
> (*Constitution of Athens* 16.9)

Order was kept in the city by Scythian archers. These slaves are believed to have been brought to Athens by Peisistratos, as they now begin regularly to adorn the vases of this period in their exotic uniforms. They survived into the heyday of the democracy, herding the citizens into the Assembly with a red-painted rope – and even being depicted in walk-on parts, and better, in the comedies of Aristophanes, where they provide a useful butt for the nimble wit of smart-talking Athenians.

The Alkmeonidai

One of the families most likely to prove a threat to Peisistratos was the Alkmeonidai. Among the most formidable of the Athenian nobility, they were active throughout the sixth century, either playing a starring role on the Athenian stage or busily stirring things behind the scenes. In the end, both Herodotus and Thucydides credited them with the liberation of Athens from tyranny. They remained influential into the fifth century, and Herodotus seems to have been on friendly terms with them – to judge by the amount of Alkmeonid history he includes in his work.

We have met them already in chapter 3 at the time of Kylon's conspiracy (c. 630 BC), when an Alkmeonid called Megakles was archon. The family came under a curse after the death of Kylon's supporters, and their rivals found this charge of sacrilege a useful stick with which to beat the Alkmeonidai at moments of crisis.

They next appear in Herodotus in the hilarious story of their enrichment by King Croesus of Lydia. After explaining that Alkmeon, son of Megakles, had helped the Lydians when they came from Sardis to consult the Delphic Oracle, Herodotus tells us how when Croesus heard of this he invited Alkmeon to Sardis and offered him as much gold as he could carry away with him.

> Alkmeon put on a large tunic with a deep fold at the front, and the widest high boots he could find, and went into the treasury to which he was taken. Attacking the heap of gold dust, he first of all stuffed his boots with as much gold as they could hold, right up to his knees, then he filled the front of his tunic full, sprinkled gold dust all over his hair, and even crammed some into his mouth. Then he staggered out of the treasury, barely able to drag his boots along and looking like nothing on earth, with his mouth stuffed full, and his body bulging all over.

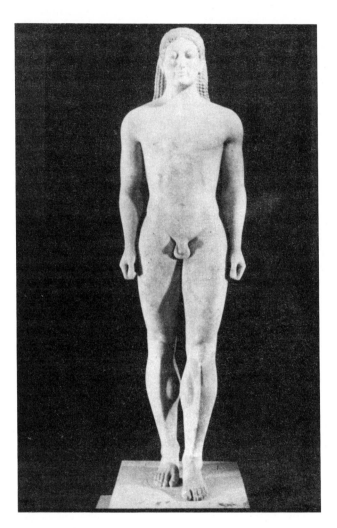

Fig. 6. Kouros from Anavyssos (the modern name for Anaphlystos: see map of Attica), about 530 BC (1.94 metres high). The inscription on the base of this statue reads 'Stop and mourn at the tomb of dead Croesus, slain in the front ranks by violent Ares'. As Anaphlystos was Alkmeonid territory, it is tempting to deduce that this statue marked the grave of an Alkmeonid killed fighting Peisistratos at the battle of Pallene. He would therefore have been named after the King of Lydia, remembered in family mythology as their earliest benefactor.

When Croesus saw him he burst out laughing and let him take all that he had, and the same amount again. This was how the family became very rich, and Alkmeon himself took up horse racing and won the chariot race at Olympia.

(HERODOTUS 6.125)

As usual with one of Herodotus' anecdotes, there are several interesting features. Chronologically the meeting between Alkmeon and Croesus is highly unlikely. But the story would serve to explain the presumably sudden enrichment of the family through doing a service to the Lydian king; and at the same time it celebrates a quick-witted Greek taking advantage of the courteous generosity of an Eastern monarch. We see an example of close contact between the aristocracies of East and West, and are reminded by the final comment that horse racing was the sport of kings even two and a half millennia ago. It is also significant to find the Alkmeonidai influential at Delphi: they kept the contact warm, and were to use it to oust the Peisistratids almost a century later.

Herodotus goes on to describe in one of his most diverting tales how the Alkmeonidai became 'much more famous still', when Megakles, son of Alkmeon, won the hand of Agariste, daughter of Kleisthenes (the tyrant of Sikyon), in the splendid Contest of the Suitors. Kleisthenes, like any proud father, wanted his daughter to marry 'the best man in the whole of Greece' and, as tyrant of Sikyon and the most recent winner of the Olympic chariot race, he presumably had a better chance than most of achieving his aim. So he invited to his palace for a year all who thought themselves worthy suitors for his daughter's hand.

The contest reminds us of the Wooing of Helen, as Herodotus, and indeed Kleisthenes, doubtless intended, for it is a conscious echo of a mythical event from the Homeric age. Herodotus names all thirteen of the contestants in a typically Homeric catalogue. They come from Italy, Epidamnos, Aetolia, Molossia, Thessaly, Euboea, Athens and various parts of the Peloponnese – all places with which Sikyon might be expected to have contact. Whether genuine or not, one can imagine these suitors' names, with those of their fathers and cities, being worked into a saga by the bard at Kleisthenes' court, and they are evidence for the easy and far-flung relationships which existed between the aristocrats of Archaic Greece.

At any rate the marriage itself must have taken place, while the details of the contest – even if it is fictional – are a fascinating insight into aristocratic life. On arrival, the suitors found that a race-track and wrestling-ground had already been prepared for the contest.

> Kleisthenes began by asking them to state their country and parentage; then, keeping them there for a year, he tested their personal prowess, temper, education and character, entering into conversation with them individually, and together in a group. He took the younger ones to the gymnasium, but the most important test of all was how they behaved at the dinner-table.
>
> (HERODOTUS 6.128)

In such a way, aristocratic hunger for competition could be satisfied in peaceful pursuits and, to sharpen the competitors' zeal, the prize was not a laurel wreath but the hand of a tyrant's daughter.

Over the year Megakles and Hippokleides, the two Athenian entrants, drew away from the rest of the field, and on the final evening, at a feast to which all the high society of Sikyon was invited, the suitors competed for the last time in 'music and conversation'. Hippokleides, 'the richest and most handsome man in Athens', was easily winning when, with wine and adrenalin flowing, he called for the music of the flute and began to dance. This proved to be his Waterloo. While Kleisthenes watched, 'with deep misgivings about the whole business', Hippokleides proceeded to dance on a table, and finally did a headstand on it waving his legs in the air.

> No longer able to restrain himself, Kleisthenes cried out, 'Son of Teisander, you have danced your marriage away!' To which Hippokleides replied, 'I couldn't care less!'
>
> (HERODOTUS 6.129)

So with Hippokleides falling at the final fence, Megakles got the girl, and his family became 'the talk of Greece'. The son of the marriage, Kleisthenes, named after his grandfather, was the man who reformed Athens into a democracy shortly after the end of the tyranny.

The Alkmeonidai and tyranny

This then is the Megakles who was leader of the coastal party in the prelude to Peisistratos' tyranny (chapter 5). A nobleman of considerable wealth and powerful connections, he joined first one side, then the other, then the first again, in his efforts to keep the Alkmeonidai in the forefront of Athenian political life.

After the battle of Pallene the family went into exile, and Herodotus claims that they remained in exile throughout the tyranny (6.123). This 'official' version of their family history endured until AD 1938, when the curtain of Alkmeonid misinformation was pulled aside by the discovery of a fragment of an archon list in the Agora:

?On]ETO[rides?

H]IPPIAS

K]LEISTHENE[s

M]ILTIADES

?Ka]LLIADE[s

?Peisi]STRAT[os

(Greek Historical Inscriptions no.6)

It is known from a literary source that Miltiades was archon in 524/3 BC, so it is possible to date the other names. Onetorides – if that is the first name – does not have any known political significance, although the name is familiar from Athenian vases, linked with the epithet *kalos* ('handsome'). He was probably appointed before Peisistratos' death in 528/7 BC, and held the archonship in 527/6 BC. It was then natural that in the following year Hippias should hold the highest office of state to mark the beginning of his reign.

Fig. 7. Fragment of an archon list from the Agora.

What is remarkable is that he was followed by the heads of the two other most powerful families in Athens. Kleisthenes, son of Megakles, must by now have returned fom exile, and his acceptance of the archonship along with that of Miltiades, one of the prominent Philaid clan (see below), would seem to indicate aristocratic acceptance of the Peisistratid dynasty. It is a reasonable conjecture that if these, the big guns of any potential opposition to the tyranny, were reconciled to Hippias, other Athenian nobles must have returned from exile with them. Kalliades was probably a member of the Kerykes, a noble family from Eleusis. The last name on the inscription would be that of Hippias' son, who dedicated the Altar of the Twelve Gods during his archonship (see chapter 7).

However, the honeymoon period soon passed. Hippias' brother was murdered in 514 BC; his reign became harsher, and the Alkmeonidai and others left Athens once again to go into open opposition. They finally succeeded in ousting the tyrants in 510 BC and, after several months of upheaval, it was Kleisthenes the Alkmeonid who found himself in control in Athens and able to put into effect the reforms which gave birth to the first-ever democracy.

The Philaidai

The other family likely to cause problems in Athens was the Philaidai, and they provide an interesting contrast with the Alkmeonidai. They claimed descent from Philaos, son of the hero Ajax, and were connected to the Kypselids, tyrants of Corinth. A Kypselos was archon of Athens in 597/6 BC, and Hippokleides, who 'couldn't care less' (p. 41), was a Philaid, his distinguished forebears giving him a head start in the eyes of Kleisthenes of Sikyon in the Contest of the Suitors (Herodotus 6.128). He became archon about ten years later (566/5 BC) in the year when the Great Panathenaia was established (see chapter 7).

Originally the Philaids came from Brauron, in the hills of north-east Attica, where the Peisistratids also owned land. As we shall see, there may have been long-standing links between the families which prevented them from coming to blows, at least during Peisistratos' lifetime.

Miltiades I is the first member of the family to appear in Herodotus' pages, and we find him installed as tyrant of the Chersonese (the Gallipoli peninsula). Herodotus describes how he came to be there:

The Dolonki of Thrace owned the Chersonese. As they were being hard pressed in a war against the Apsinthians, they sent their rulers to Delphi to consult the oracle. The Priestess told them that they should take back home with them, to put their affairs in order, the first man who invited them in and entertained them after they left the temple. The Dolonki went off along the Sacred Road and passed through Phocis and Boeotia, and when nobody asked them in, they turned aside to Athens.

Peisistratos was the most powerful man in Athens at that time, but Miltiades, the son of Kypselos, also enjoyed considerable influence. He came from a family which had the means to enter a team for the Olympic chariot race. Sitting in his porch, Miltiades happened to see the Dolonki going by, wearing foreign clothes and carrying spears, so he called to them, and when they came near he offered them shelter and hospitality. They accepted his offer, and while they were in his house they told him all about the oracle, and then begged him to follow the God's advice. When Miltiades heard this he agreed at once to go with them, for in fact he was feeling frustrated with Peisistratos' rule, and wanted to leave Athens. So he straight away sent to Delphi to ask if he was right to do what the Dolonki asked of him.

The Priestess gave her approval, and so Miltiades, the son of Kypselos – who had previously won the Olympic four-horse chariot race – gathered together any Athenians who wanted to be part of the expedition, and set sail with the Dolonki. He proceeded to take charge of their land, and the chiefs who had brought him back made him their tyrant.

(HERODOTUS 6.34-36)

Some of the details of this story are too good to be true, and it is likely that much of it was concocted later as an *apologia*, at a time when it was less fashionable to have tyrants in the family tree. However, it is not hard to see how everyone concerned benefited from the outcome. Miltiades gained freedom for the self-expression required of a man of his breeding. Winning chariot races was all very well, but to rule as tyrant in his own right among the warring tribes of the Chersonese was really hitting the jackpot. Peisistratos, on the other hand, could now breathe more freely the air of an Athens devoid of a potentially dangerous rival. Whether the original request for a colony came from Athens or from the Dolonki themselves, they gained a strong leader and his followers, who gave them security from their neighbours. The authority of Delphi is the mainspring of the story as told by Herodotus; but even if this seal of religious approval was added later, for public consumption, it is a reminder of how seriously Greeks regarded such authority.

As far as relations between the rival Athenians are concerned, it seems clear that Miltiades could not have taken the colonists without Peisistratos' approval, and that Peisistratos would not have encouraged an enemy to hold such a strategic position on the bank of the Hellespont.

Once there, Miltiades built a wall to keep out the Apsinthians and then, by attacking Lampsakos, on the opposite shore of the strait, began a struggle which lasted for years. In the course of it, he was captured by the Lampsakenes and only set free when King Croesus threatened them with total destruction. This incident, which must have happened before Croesus was defeated by the Persians in 546 BC, makes it very likely that Miltiades went out to the Chersonese during one of Peisistratos' first two periods of tyranny.

The Dolonki themselves were satisfied with Miltiades' record. Herodotus tells how a century later they were still holding in his honour the sacrifices 'due to the founder of a state, with chariot-racing and athletic competitions, which nobody from Lampsakos is allowed to enter' (6.38). It was a suitably Homeric memorial.

His successor in power was Stesagoras, the son of his half-brother Kimon, and he perished in the war against Lampsakos. On his death, the sons of Peisistratos sent his brother Miltiades II out to take his place, sometime after he had been archon in 524/3 BC. He wasted no time in asserting himself.

> On arriving in the Chersonese Miltiades stayed at home, apparently out of respect for his dead brother. When they heard this, the leading men from all the cities of the Chersonese gathered together and came in a body to mourn with him. Miltiades promptly imprisoned them all. That was how he became ruler of the Chersonese; he kept a bodyguard of 500 mercenaries, and married Hegesipyle, the daughter of the Thracian King Oloros.
>
> (HERODOTUS 6.39.2)

It is interesting to note that another Oloros, perhaps the son of this princess by a second marriage, was the father of the historian

Thucydides. The world of the archaic aristocracy was, in many ways, a small one.

There are some uncertainties about the subsequent career of Miltiades II. He fell foul of the western advance of the Persian Empire, and may have spent some years in exile. Eventually he returned to Athens in 493 BC, escaping from the dying embers of the Ionian Revolt, and was immediately taken to court by 'his enemies' – no prizes for guessing who they might be – and charged with being a tyrant in the Chersonese (Herodotus 6.104). He was acquitted and, shortly after, as one of the ten elected generals, masterminded the Athenian victory over the Persians at Marathon.

It is in the context of the battle of Marathon that Herodotus tells us about the head of the Philaids back in Greece, Miltiades' father Kimon, nicknamed Koalemos ('Dimwit').

> He was exiled from Athens by Peisistratos, and when in exile he won the Olympic four-horse chariot race, as his half-brother Miltiades had done. In the next Olympic Games he won the race again with the same team and allowed the victory to be announced in Peisistratos' name. For this he was granted permission to return to his family estates. But when, after the death of Peisistratos, he won a third victory, still with the same team, the sons of the tyrant sent hired assassins who killed him by night near the Council Chamber. He is buried outside the city, on the other side of the Hollow Road, and opposite him are buried the mares which won the three Olympic victories.
>
> (HERODOTUS 6.103.2-3)

It is a sad tale, although the end is touching. As far as we know, Kimon played no direct part in political life, and his nickname suggests that in himself he was unlikely to be a threat to Peisistratos. Nevertheless, his powerful family and his success at the races were enough for Peisistratos to send him into exile (the exact date is unknown). He won his third Olympic victory in 528 BC, the year of Peisistratos' death. It is an indication of how edgy the tyrants' sons must then have been feeling that they should have ordered Kimon's murder; perhaps, ironically, as he left the Council Chamber after the free dinner which was his right as an Olympic champion. If they really were responsible, as Herodotus claims, they must have covered their tracks successfully, at least to begin with, for Miltiades II agreed to be archon in 524/3 BC, and went off with their blessing to the Chersonese soon afterwards.

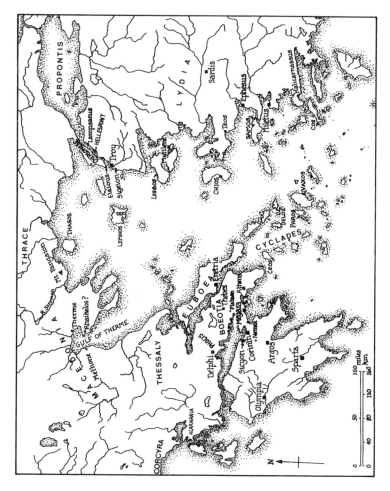

Fig. 8. Map of Greece and the Aegean.

It is instructive to see how the tyrants dealt with these two families, who in one way or another posed a constant threat to them. Peisistratos seems to have had a firmer and surer touch than his sons, and perhaps Hippias' olive branch, the archonships of Kleisthenes and Miltiades, can be seen with hindsight to have been a mistake. Did the rivals hurry back to Athens, with an eye to the main chance, as soon as they heard of the old tyrant's death? Was Hippias perhaps stampeded into a gesture of reconciliation he did not have the strength of character to carry through? Wherever the truth lies, other events beyond Hippias' control (see chapter 9) were conspiring to hurry the tyranny to its close.

If there was some sort of alliance originally between the Peisistratids and the Philaidai, this might explain why the Philaids were content to work with the tyranny – enjoying their own tyrannical power abroad – while the Alkmeonids were more inclined to go into open opposition. On the other hand, if the story of Alkmeon and Croesus is intended to suggest a whiff of the nouveau riche about the family, then their extravagant spending on race-horses, their marrying into powerful families, and their ability to sniff out any wind of change and capitalise on it, are certainly the actions of a family eager to make its mark – both in politics and prestige. In a way, the Philaids seem more self-confident and secure, except for poor Kimon ('Dimwit') and his remarkable mares. It is significant that we never read of the Peisistratids breeding race-horses: they had no need to.

Naxos and Delos

Peisistratos proved to be as imaginative and sure-footed in his foreign relations as he was in his handling of home affairs. The part played by Lygdamis of Naxos in Peisistratos' victory at Pallene has been described in chapter 5. The two exiles probably met in Eretria – Lygdamis too had enjoyed a short spell as tyrant – and Peisistratos rewarded him for his help in 546 BC by driving out the ruling oligarchy from Naxos immediately afterwards and reinstating Lygdamis as tyrant.

'Bright Naxos', as Pindar calls it, the largest and most fertile of the Cyclades Islands, was famous for its marble and its sculptors – like Paros, a close neighbour and long-standing rival. Lygdamis, who may have shared Peisistratos' somewhat blunt sense of humour, is said to have raised money by confiscating half-finished statues on the island and offering to sell them to the original patrons, or to the highest bidder. He also 'allowed' exiled aristocrats to buy back their own land.

In about 532 BC he helped Polykrates of Samos to seize power, thus, in theory at least, extending Athenian influence right across the Aegean. There is no clear evidence that Peisistratos helped him in this, although Athens and Samos had a common enemy in Mytilene, later defeated at sea by Polykrates (Herodotus 3.39.4).

Lygdamis was expelled by a Spartan force in 517 BC, but Naxos continued to flourish under the oligarchy imposed by Sparta, while its fleet dominated the southern Aegean in the vacuum left by the death of Polykrates (in about 523 BC). It beat off a Persian attack in 500 BC, at the beginning of the Ionian Revolt, and was described at the time by Herodotus as 'the richest of the islands' (5.28).

Apollo is said to have been born on Delos, and the island enjoyed an importance out of all proportion to its size through being the centre of the cult of Apollo for the Ionian Greeks. Its ruins reflect the interest taken in it by a succession of powerful neighbours. There are colossal pieces of statuary (including fragments of a *kouros* almost ten metres high, see p. 76), dedicated by Naxians in the seventh and early sixth centuries, and Peisistratos used his alliance with Lygdamis to move in and stamp the influence of Athens on Delos.

> In response to an oracle, he purified the island of Delos in the following manner: he dug up all the bodies which were buried within sight of the temple and transferred them to another part of the island.
>
> (HERODOTUS 1.64)

He also had the temple of Apollo rebuilt in Attic limestone around 540 BC. Such confident gestures by the tyrant of Athens would hardly go unnoticed by the many Ionians who visited the sanctuary every year.

Polykrates of Samos was not to be outdone. In the 520s he seized the nearby island of Rheneia and actually joined it to Delos by a chain as an offering to Apollo!

Sigeion

In the northern Aegean, Athenian intervention in the Thracian Chersonese has already been discussed. Towards the end of the seventh century settlers had gone out to two other towns in that area – Sigeion on the south side of the strait and Elaious on the north, right at the point where the waters of the Propontis emerge into the Aegean Sea. The area had been colonised earlier by settlers from Mytilene, a *polis* on the island of Lesbos, and they fought Athens over it for the next seventy years.

The story went that the Athenian founder, Phrynon, an Olympic victor of 636/5 BC, was killed in a duel with the Mytilenean champion Pittakos in 607/6 BC – a nice Homeric touch. This cannot have settled the matter, however, for Periander, the tyrant of Corinth (who died in 585 BC), was called in later to arbitrate, and he awarded Sigeion to Athens. It was during this fighting that the poet Alkaios wryly relates in a famous fragment how he escaped with his life, but not his shield, which the Athenians took and hung up in the temple of Athene in Sigeion.

Some time afterwards Athens must have lost Sigeion, for Herodotus tells how Peisistratos 'took it by force from the Mytileneans' and installed as tyrant his son Hegesistratos, who had to defend the outpost against subsequent Mytilenean attacks. (In his account (5.94-5), Herodotus seems to have conflated two separate wars, those of Phrynon and Peisistratos, for he makes Periander the arbitrator in Peisistratos' lifetime, which is chronologically impossible).

The benefits of having a friendly *polis* on both sides of the Hellespont must have been considerable. Even if the original colonists went partly to get away from Athens (perhaps for political reasons), the care taken by Peisistratos to ensure a continuing Athenian presence in this area, and indeed the whole of the Chersonese, is remarkable. It has often been said that this was done to safeguard the Athenian corn supply from the Black Sea, but there is no evidence for regular shipments of corn from this area as early as the sixth century. Possession of Sigeion and Elaious ensured that Athenian sailors had a friendly (and cheap) harbour in which to shelter while they waited for the prevailing north wind to change and let them sail up the Propontis. It also gave them the opportunity to interfere with the ships of other states in the Hellespont. However, Peisistratos' main aim was probably to make sure his family had their own possessions abroad.

In time, the shadow of Persia fell across these Athenian outposts, and the sons of Peisistratos seem to have continued their rule in Sigeion with the blessing of the Great King. Such a link with the enemy did not endear them to the ever-vigilant King Kleomenes of Sparta, especially when Hippias married his daughter to the son of

Hippoklos, tyrant of Lampsakos and friend of Darius. When Apollo urged the Spartans to liberate Athens (see p. 86), the appeal did not fall on deaf ears. In 510 BC, ousted by the Spartan army, Hippias and his family retired to Sigeion. It is ironic to see how the focus of Peisistratos' adventurous pro-Athenian interest in the north-east may, with the march of Persia towards the West, have become a motive for his son's expulsion from Athens. At least it provided a haven for them in their exile.

Mainland Greece

In summarising Peisistratos' foreign policy, mention must also be made of his strong links with Argos. He had married Timonassa, daughter of an Argive called Gorgilos, around the time of his first tyranny, and this Argive connection, as we have seen, produced mercenaries to fight at Pallene. The tyrants must have carried on their friendship with Thebes: a *kouros* dedicated by Hipparchos has been found in the shrine of Apollo Ptoos in Boeotia, twenty kilometres north of Thebes.

Thessaly too remained an ally, as may be seen from the name of another of Peisistratos' sons, Thessalos (he was probably a separate person from Hegesistratos, despite *Constitution of Athens* 17.3), and the fact that the Thessalian war-chieftain Kineas came with a thousand cavalry to help Hippias defeat the invasion of Anchimolios (Herodotus 5.63.2). They also offered him the city of Iolkos on his final departure from Athens (ibid. 5.94.1).

Finally, the area around the River Strymon with its silver mines presumably continued to supply revenue, while Macedonia (Peisistratos had settled in nearby Rhaikelos during his ten-year exile) remained friendly enough for their King Amyntas to offer Hippias a place of refuge in 510 BC (ibid. 5.94.1).

'He doth bestride the narrow world...'

Peisistratos was hardly a world conqueror in Julius Caesar's mould. Yet in dealing firmly with his rivals at home, and maintaining useful connections with other parts of mainland Greece, he provided the settled conditions necessary for taking positive action abroad. The approaches to the Black Sea saw a continuing Athenian presence even after Persia took over the area, while Peisistratos' close alliance with Lygdamis of Naxos ensured a strong Athenian influence in the south

Aegean. These policies were given strength and purpose by two underlying themes.

Solon had described Athens as 'the oldest land of Ionia', and her citizens themselves believed that they lived in the mother city of all the Ionian *poleis* on the Aegean islands and down the coast of Asia Minor. There was probably much truth in this. Many emigrants would have passed through Attica en route for the east; but of course other cities sent their settlers too.

In the overseas activities of Peisistratos, especially on Delos, we can see Athens reaching out to make a decisive claim for the leadership of the Ionian Greeks; and it is not too much to say that Peisistratos pointed the way towards the Athenian Empire of the fifth century.

The other theme is the Homeric one. In this chapter we have seen the nobility of Athens vying for power. Once he had gained control of Athens for his own family, Peisistratos was able to strive for excellence in a wider arena. Using his extensive network of friends and allies and backed by the wealth and enterprise of a thriving *polis*, he could compete on an international scale. Polykrates of Samos, the colourful piratical tyrant (only briefly mentioned above) was a worthy and typical rival whose grandiose building surely inspired the sons of Peisistratos (chapter 7), as he was himself inspired by Athenian devotion on Delos.

This is the Contest of the Suitors writ large. With the spread of heroic ideals, and a web of relationships connecting aristocrats and tyrants across land and sea, the whole Greek world was drawn into a huge Homeric *agon* (contest). The rewards for the winners in prestige, wealth and power, were enormous.

Chapter 7
The Golden Age

'They made the city beautiful...' *(Thucydides)*

In Mycenean times the Greeks had built palaces and tombs for their kings. As the *poleis* emerged from the chrysalis of the Dark Age, tentatively spreading their wings, one way in which they began to show their colours was by building temples for their gods. This act of piety not only provided shelter for the images of the gods who protected their cities, but also promoted unity among the citizens who worshipped together. From Sicily to Ionia the temples rose during the eighth century. The earliest ones were made of wood, but the wealthy Corinthians, who seem to have been innovators in this field, were the first to build early in the seventh century a temple with walls of dressed stone and a tiled roof. This has not survived, but their colony Kerkyra on the island of Corfu built in about 580 BC the first temple entirely of stone, and the first we know of to have sculptures in its pediments: the striking Gorgon with her attendant panthers.

As aristocracies yielded to tyrannies, the new rulers were not slow to see the possibilities for self-advertisement and competition in monumental architecture. The temple of Artemis at Ephesus, built around 550 BC, was more than twice the size of the Parthenon, which was built a century later. Polykrates, tyrant of Samos, brought to completion what Herodotus describes as 'the largest of all known temples' (3.60.4) around 530 BC.

Peisistratos and his family did not fail to take up the gauntlet thus flung before them by their fellow-tyrants in the East. Although we rightly think of Pericles' building programme (447 BC onwards) as one of Athens' finest achievements, the standard had been set by the tyrants a century earlier. Thanks to the post-Solonian boom, and the arrival of Peisistratos, Athens now enjoyed two essential prerequisites for public building on a monumental scale: an accumulation of wealth, and a strong central authority. She already had a good supply of marble, and the combination of these factors ushered in the first great period of building in Athenian history.

Unfortunately, some of what they built was destroyed by the

Persians in 480 BC, and much else has perished. But archaeological remains and literary references help us to piece together a picture of the striking transformation in their city's appearance which the people of Athens must have enjoyed in the second half of the sixth century. There are also problems in dating the different developments: the best clues are usually afforded by pottery discovered in the foundations, and by the building techniques and materials used. It is therefore hard to know whether to attribute the initiative to Peisistratos or to his sons. An upward curve is nevertheless clearly discernible, from Peisistratos' comparatively modest improvements to the Agora, through the series of imposing fountain-houses and the renovation of the temple on the Acropolis, to the grandiose but doomed ambition of the Olympieion in the final years.

The development of the Agora as a civic centre has already been mentioned, and it was here, where the roads meet, that Peisistratos continued to build. The public area of the Agora, to judge by the filling of wells and the demolition of houses, seems to have been gradually extended to the east and south between 575 BC and 525 BC. One building, erected about 550-525 BC and of irregular shape, with many rooms grouped round two sides of a colonnaded courtyard, looks like a rather grand private house, and may well have been the home of Peisistratos and his family. A religious dimension was added to the Agora by the installation of two cults: to Zeus Agoraios (Zeus of the Agora) and to Apollo Patroos (Ancestral Apollo), represented by shrines on the west side of the square.

In the south-east corner of the Agora the foundations have been discovered of a fountain-house dating to 530-520 BC. The terracotta pipes bringing water underground from the east have also survived. Another, dating from the same period, has been found south-west of the Areiopagos in a residential area. Thucydides refers (2.15.5) to a fountain-house – the famous *Enneakrounos* (Nine-spouter) – as one of the works of the tyrants; it was probably situated south-east of the Acropolis.

Other tyrants improved the water supply for their cities by building aqueducts and fountain-houses, for instance in Megara and Corinth. Herodotus mentions with admiration (3.60) the tunnel built through a mountain on Samos to take water to the city, which Aristotle attributed to the tyrant Polykrates (*Politics* 1313b). In building such amenities the tyrants made themselves popular by providing a ready supply of fresh water, easily collected in a jar filled at a spout, rather than drawn from a deep well. They also provided a congenial social centre for the women, as can be seen from the many vases of this period depicting fountain-house scenes.

More than half concealed by the modern railway, the Altar of the Twelve Gods lies on the north side of the Agora. (Excavators in AD 1946 had regularly to beat a hasty retreat in the face of passing trains!) Thucydides tells us (6.54.6) that it was dedicated by Peisistratos' grandson, also named Peisistratos, during his archonship; and a fragment of an archon list found in the Agora dates this to 522/1 BC, during his father Hippias' tyranny (see p. 42). This altar must have been the hub of the road-system which the tyrants are said to have built in Attica, as a reference in Herodotus (2.7) shows that it was regarded as the central point in Athens from which distances were measured – rather like Charing Cross in London. This is an indication of the importance which the Peisistratids attached to the Agora as the heart of the city.

Today, when you have passed through the Propylaia, the 'entrance' or 'gateway' to the Acropolis, the view is dominated by the Parthenon on your right, and the Erechtheion on your left. Neither of these existed in the sixth century BC. At that time you would have seen before you a temple whose foundations are still visible, immediately to the south of the Erechtheion and parallel to it, with part of its wall actually running below the Caryatid porch of the Erechtheion. This was a temple to Athene Polias (Guardian of the City), and is mentioned by Herodotus as the temple where the Peisistratids had kept some oracles and which King Kleomenes of Sparta sacrilegiously entered in 508 BC (Herodotus 5.90 and 72). The temple was of limestone and most likely begun, if not completed, before 546 BC when Peisistratos finally established himself as tyrant.

There is much controversy over the sixth-century buildings on the Acropolis, which were sacked by the Persians in 480 BC. When the Athenians returned afterwards they piled all the statues, which had been knocked down, in pits on the Acropolis, and the discovery of these last century provided us with a matchless collection of sixth century sculpture (see chapter 8). There are more pieces of pedimental sculpture than are needed to adorn a single temple, and in view of their developing styles it is generally agreed that the existing temple of Athene Polias was improved about 520 BC and given new sets of sculptures.

It has been suggested that Peisistratos actually lived on the

Acropolis during his rule. The evidence for this is that very few aristocratic dedications have been found there which date from before his death, while there are plenty from the following years, and it is argued that he forbade dedications while he had his home there. This cannot be proved; but other tyrants lived in strongholds, and Peisistratos may have felt safer there, while his sons had the confidence to leave the Acropolis after their father died.

Fig. 9. The foundations of the archaic temple to Athene Polias on the Acropolis, with the 5th century Erechtheion in the background. These are known as the Dörpfeld foundations, after the German archaeologist who discovered them in AD 1885.

Other religious building took place at Eleusis (see below), where the increasing popularity of the cult of Demeter required a larger hall for the celebration of the mysteries. Some time soon after 550 BC a temple was built to Athene at Sounion, the predecessor of the Poseidon temple whose ruins grace the promontory today. Peisistratos' activity on the island of Delos, where he 'cleansed' the island shortly after 546 BC and built or restored the temple of Apollo, is discussed in chapter 6.

Potentially the most spectacular building undertaken by the tyrants was the Olympieion, or temple to Olympian Zeus, situated half a mile south-east of the Acropolis. This was started by Peisistratos' sons in about 520 BC and was clearly intended to rival the huge temples at Ephesus and Samos. Had it been completed, it would have been the largest temple on the Greek mainland, measuring 107.75 by 41.10 metres, and more than twice the size of the temple to Athene Polias on the Acropolis. Unfortunately, the Peisistratids were expelled when only the foundations and the first column drums were in place, and the work was discontinued. Presumably the Athenians, labouring to give birth to democracy, had little inclination to spend vast sums of money on a monument to the late departed tyrants. Perhaps not unexpectedly, it was left to two later autocrats to carry on the building: King Antiochus of Syria (175-164 BC) changed from the Doric to the much more ornate Corinthian order when he restarted the work, and the temple was eventually completed by the Roman Emperor Hadrian, who dedicated it in AD 131/2.

Aristotle (*Politics* 1313b9) loftily says that tyrants instigated public works programmes to keep their subjects occupied and poor, citing as examples the Pyramids of Egypt, Polykrates' buildings on Samos, and the Olympieion in Athens. But this is only part of the story. In fact the Athenian building presumably provided jobs, as did Pericles' programme a hundred years later. Rivalry has already been mentioned as a motive, and the competitive spirit of the Peisistratids must surely have been fuelled by the temple of Apollo in neighbouring Corinth, built about 540 BC, whose seven remaining columns – the only surviving sixth century temple in Greece – still dominate the ruins of the Agora in Corinth today.

In addition, the spate of projects begun around 520 BC, just after Peisistratos' death, might also be explained by the need of the second generation of tyrants to make their mark, both at home and abroad, with some spectacular and popular achievements.

A final motive, provided by Peisistratos from the start, was the unification of Attica. The Agora was upgraded as a political centre, the worship of Athene was encouraged on the Acropolis and in festivals, until gradually Athens became the focal point for all citizens. Solon wrote that Athene protects Athens, 'her hands stretched out over our heads', and there must have been much genuine religious feeling in her worship. But it cannot be denied that Athens, and the Peisistratids, stood to gain quite a lot as well.

The Great Panathenaia

In their religion the Greeks were more concerned with correct practice than correct belief, and festivals played a very important part in this religious activity. Festivals brought the citizen body together in a communal activity, and never so closely as when they met to worship the patron god or goddess of their *polis*. Towards the end of July every summer the Athenians celebrated the birthday of Athene, their patron goddess, in a festival called the Panathenaia (Festival of All Athens).

It was originally the occasion when a new *peplos* (robe) was handed over to the goddess for her cult statue (an image of olive wood), and had begun in the seventh century or earlier. In the sixth century, however, the festival took on new dimensions. Athletic contests were added to it every four years, and this enlarged celebration was now called the Great Panathenaia, to distinguish it from the lesser festivals in the intervening years. The traditional date for this innovation was 566/5 BC when Hippokleides, a member of the Philaid family, was archon.

It is impossible to discern the political significance in Athens itself of this religious expansion in the restless years immediately before Peisistratos' first bid for the tyranny. In the broader Greek context, however, it is an interesting development. The Olympic Games were Greece's premier sporting festival, held in honour of Zeus himself. They had been founded in the eighth century and were followed by the Pythian Games (582 BC), the Isthmian Games (581 BC) and the Nemean Games (573 BC). The enlargement of the Panathenaia looks very like an attempt by the Athenians to join the top league of Greek religious centres which held important quadrennial games.

The next development in the Panathenaia is specifically linked to the tyrants. Hipparchos, Peisistratos' son, was said to have 'brought the words of Homer' to Athens and established competitive recitations of the *Iliad* and the *Odyssey* by *rhapsodoi* (minstrels) as part of the festival. For this, and all the other competitions, prizes were given consisting of olive oil in large *amphorae* (two-handled storage jars). The poet Pindar, writing of a successful wrestler later in the century, describes how he had received as a prize 'in earth baked by the fire, the fruit of the olive, in highly decorated jars.'

The highlight of the Panathenaia was the procession in which various groups representing a cross-section of the people of Athens escorted the *peplos* along the Panathenaic Way through the Agora and up on to the Acropolis. Parts of this grand and solemn procession are depicted on the frieze of the Parthenon, carved the following century. The festival was then rounded off by a huge sacrifice and a feast which all the citizens shared. The excellence of this repast is touched on by Socrates in Aristophanes' comedy *Clouds* (lines 386-7) when as an illustration of the working of thunder he asks his pupil 'Have you ever filled yourself with soup at the Panathenaia, then had a stomach upset and felt a sudden loud rumbling inside?'

The Great Dionysia

Aristotle said that in holding festivals men 'pay to the gods the honour that is their due, and at the same time provide pleasant relaxation for themselves.' Another festival which combined these two characteristics, and which was traditionally enhanced by the Peisistratids, was the Great or City Dionysia – so called to distinguish it from the other Dionysia held in various parts of Attica. It had its roots in the soil, like so many festivals, and was held in the spring in honour of Dionysos, the god of fertility and wine. It had originally been celebrated in Eleutherai, a small village on the northern border of Attica, near Thebes, but was later moved to Athens at a time when Eleutherai preferred the protection of Athens to that of Thebes. This origin was commemorated each year by taking the wooden image of Dionysos out of the city to a shrine on the road to Thebes, where it remained for several days before being escorted back to Athens with appropriate ceremony.

It is not certain when the festival was transferred to Athens, but the fact that it was run by the *archon eponymos*, rather than the *basileus*, suggests a comparatively late date, and it would be fully in keeping with Peisistratos' policy of centralisation for the move to have taken place at some time during the tyranny.

The festival proper began with a grand procession, which was the central rite, and, as in the Panathenaia, a representative assortment of citizens took part. Some carried models of erect phalluses, the traditional fertility symbol; others bore leather bottles of wine, offerings of first-fruits to the god; others drove the bulls for the sacrifice. This was followed by a feast and, to end the day, a huge *komos* (revel) through the city. The morning after, ritual performances of mumming, singing and dancing were held in the Agora, and it was from these unlikely beginnings that Greek drama, indeed the very concept of the theatre, eventually grew. (The word 'comedy' appears to be derived from the singing which accompanied the *komos*).

This development can be more definitely attributed to Peisistratos' reign. A third century inscription tells us that a certain Thespis, probably in 534 BC, 'first' acted and produced a play in Athens, and won a goat (*tragos*) as a prize. Some confirmation of this date is provided by the traces of buildings dating to the late sixth century which have been found underneath the fourth century Theatre of Dionysos on the southern slope of the Acropolis. They consist of a round dancing-floor (*orchestra*) for singers and dancers, with a small shrine behind, and a hollowed-out semi-circle for the audience.

Thespis, whoever he was, and Peisistratos, whatever his part (if any) in this development, could hardly have foreseen the mighty oak which was to grow from so small – and to us so shadowy – an acorn. This is not the place for a discussion of the origins of Greek tragedy. Nevertheless, it all started in Athens at about this time; and if tragedy and comedy are among the Greeks' most precious legacies to mankind, then some credit must go to the tyrant who ruled Athens during these years.

The competitive nature of the drama should also be noted. The Greek word for a contest of any kind, athletic or dramatic, was *agon* (from which the word 'agony' is derived). The leading actor was called the *protagonistes* which literally means 'first competitor', and in the fifth century there was keen competition for the prizes which were awarded to the winning plays, actors and producers. Thus the most sacred religious occasions were shot through with the rivalry which was, in part, the Greeks' inheritance from the Homeric heroes of old.

Eleusis and elsewhere

Mention has already been made of the building of a new and larger *Telesterion* (Hall of Mysteries) at Eleusis. This has traditionally been attributed to Peisistratos, although the evidence is inconclusive. What is known is that the Mysteries of Demeter, the goddess of the corn crop – originally a local cult at Eleusis – grew much more popular during the sixth century. At the same time Athens became decisively involved in the celebrations, to judge by the offerings found on the site of the fifth century Eleusinion in Athens. In this festival, holy objects were brought from Eleusis to Athens and lodged in the Eleusinion, a sacred place on the slope between the Agora and the Acropolis. Then a great procession involving the initiates and many other pilgrims, the priests of the cult, and a military escort, made its way over the fourteen miles to Eleusis where the initiation ceremony was held.

It seems that Athens may have tried to take over this cult completely but failed, and the resultant compromise shows Athens playing an important, yet subsidiary part in the festival as a whole, which was still firmly based at Eleusis.

Artemis had long been worshipped at Brauron, where the Peisistratid family came from. In the fifth century there was a precinct to Artemis of Brauron on the Acropolis, just inside the Propylaia, consisting of an altar and a stoa (portico). It is not known when it was built, but it is a reasonable assumption that the tyrants first established a sacred place on the Acropolis for the Artemis of their home village.

Peisistratos' religious interests even extended across the sea to the island of Delos. His actions there, and the strong political motive behind them, are described in chapter 6.

Despite some uncertainties, several strands can be seen running through the various religious activities of Peisistratos and his sons. There is the centralisation of cults: Athens either took over or took part in what had formerly been local festivals, so that their local significance vanished, or was outshone by the central celebration. Besides, a festival like the Panathenaia actually glorified Athens, for in it, although competitors came from all over Greece, the Athenians were merged into a single body of celebrants setting themselves apart from other Greeks, just as in the international festivals the Greeks set themselves apart from other mortals.

Festivals were social occasions at which citizens enjoyed themselves and did things together; but there was also a striving for excellence in all the competitions. This honoured the god or goddess, and also set higher standards for the citizens to aim for the following year. During the fourth and third centuries BC at least 120 days in the year were devoted to festivals in Athens, and the city was said to have had twice as many festivals as any other *polis* (partly, of course, because Attica originally had many separate communities). For the merging together of so many cults and the encouraging of a tradition of so many colourful and splendid occasions, the tyrants appear to have been largely responsible.

Taxes and laws

So much for the outward show: the grand state occasions and the monumental architecture which were, among other things, a splendid attempt to stake Athens' claim to the headship of the Ionian Greeks. But what of the man in the street? What was the effect of the tyranny on his daily life?

Chapter 16 of the *Constitution of Athens* consists of a fascinating collection of facts, anecdotes and comments which show us something of the nuts and bolts of Peisistratos' rule and his dealings with the ordinary Athenian. The picture is entirely favourable, and [Aristotle] is moved to quote 'a common saying that the tyranny of Peisistratos was the Age of Kronos; for later, when his sons took over, the rule became much harsher.' (In Greek myth, the Age of Kronos, the father of Zeus, was a Golden Age.)

[Aristotle] deals first with Peisistratos and the farmers:

> Peisistratos organised affairs in the city with moderation, more like a citizen than a tyrant. He was generally humane and mild and inclined to show mercy to wrongdoers, and in particular he used to lend money to those who were in difficulties, to help them with their work so that they could continue supporting themselves by farming. He did this for two reasons: so that they should not spend time in the city but should be scattered throughout the countryside; and so that they should have sufficient of the necessities of life and be concerned with their private affairs, and so have neither the desire nor the leisure to get involved in public affairs. At the same time he found that his revenues became greater as the land was being properly worked, for he levied a tithe on the produce.
>
> (*Constitution of Athens* 16.2-4)

Autocrats from the beginning of time have kept their subjects busy to prevent them plotting together, but perhaps the writer here is rather too eager to give his theories on tyranny an airing. It would be in the interests of everyone for struggling peasants to be given some assistance, especially if it were to encourage them to change from growing cereals to cultivating olives and vines, which are in the long run more profitable. It has been suggested that Peisistratos distributed among small farmers the land of his defeated opponents, but there is no evidence for this.

The wherewithal for these loans would come from taxes. [Aristotle] mentions a tithe on produce, but he may be using a general term for tax and not mean 10% specifically, for Thucydides (6.54.5) says that the tyrants levied a 5% tax 'only', and even if he is referring to Peisistratos' sons, it seems unlikely that they reduced the tax in view of their ambitious building enterprises. Herodotus also mentions (1.64) Peisistratos' revenue from property on the River Strymon, and it is probable that there was in practice little distinction between taxes officially raised and the tyrants' personal income from various sources.

As an example of Peisistratos the generous man of the people, [Aristotle] recounts the following anecdote:

> The story goes that when Peisistratos was on one of his tours of the countryside there occurred the incident involving the man who was farming what was later called Tax-Free Farm. He saw a man digging and working at what was nothing but rock, and in his amazement told his slave to ask the man what he got from his land. 'Nothing but troubles and pains,' came the reply, 'and of these troubles and pains Peisistratos must take a tithe.' The man gave his answer without knowing who he was talking to, and Peisistratos, delighted by his plain speaking and his hard work, let him off all taxes.
>
> (*Constitution of Athens* 16.6)

In view of the fact that Peisistratos was actually remitting his share of the 'troubles and pains', the story perhaps tells us more about Peisistratos' sense of humour than his generosity.

This incident, we are told, took place on one of Peisistratos' tours of the countryside:

> For this reason (i.e. to keep the people busy) he instituted village judges, and he himself also often used to go out into the country to make inspections and to settle disputes so that men would not come into the city and neglect their work.
>
> (*Constitution of Athens* 16.5)

A good ruler gets to know his people, and it is clear from this and other examples that Peisistratos did not lack the common touch. Another benefit to him from these travelling judges would be that people in the countryside became more dependent on the official sent by Peisistratos from the city, and so the influence of the local aristocrat, already severely weakened by Peisistratos' very existence, would wane still further.

Herodotus, Thucydides and [Aristotle] all agree in saying that the tyrants did not upset the existing constitution but continued to administer everything according to the laws. It was Athens' good fortune that these laws had been laid down by as wise and humane a reformer as Solon. [Aristotle] adds an illustration:

> He wanted to run everything according to the laws, not making himself superior to anyone else; and once, when he was summoned to appear before the Areiopagos on a charge of murder he came forward himself to make his defence, but his accuser took fright, and failed to appear.
>
> (*Constitution of Athens* 16.8)

Under this rule of law, administered by a benevolent and fair ruler, and enjoying peace at home, Athens prospered. We have seen what strides she took in the years following Solon's reforms, and this progress continued.

Trade and coinage

Encouraged no doubt by Peisistratos' many overseas contacts, trade increased. Athens had cornered the world market for black-figure vases by 550 BC, and she was now reaping the rewards of this predominance. An artistic result was the boldness of the enterprising artists who began in about 530 BC to experiment with red-figure, and quickly mastered the new technique. And it must never be forgotten that exported vases held something – usually high quality Attic oil. Innumerable vases, found all round the Mediterranean, testify to the extent of Attic trade, and the pictures on them reveal a confident, developing society enjoying an increasing range of fine, even luxurious, goods. This growth was strongly encouraged by Peisistratos' energetic activities both in mainland Greece and abroad.

It is now generally agreed that the Athenians began minting silver coins during the tyranny. The first to appear have been called Wappenmünzen ('heraldic coins'), after the various designs on the obverse which were once thought to be the badges of different aristocratic families. More recently, these designs have been explained by the theory that when Athenians began to mint for themselves, they were influenced by their Ionian connections (and Peisistratos' Aegean contacts), because eastern Greek coinages show a similar variety in their early stages. A migration of Ionian artists and craftsmen is to be expected in the years following the conquest of the Ionian Greek *poleis* by King Croesus of Lydia (where coinage was invented, according to Herodotus 1.94), and later, when Lydia itself

Fig. 10. (a) This example of a 'heraldic coin' shows a Gorgon's head on the obverse, with a lion's head and paws on the reverse.

(b) A typical archaic 'owl'. The obverse has the head of Athene; the reverse has an owl, an olive branch, and the letters A TH E.

fell to the Persians.

These early coins were soon succeeded by the well-known 'owls' of Athens, and analysis of the types suggests a different origin for the silver of each. It is an unproveable, but attractive theory that the earlier coins were minted with silver from Peisistratos' Thracian mines, until the standard 'owls' could be produced using silver from Athens' own mines at Laurion in south-east Attica.

When the change took place is uncertain. But whether Hippias, or the new democracy, stamped the head of Athene on one side and her sacred bird, the owl, on the other, they were symbolising to the world the new wealth and success of her city. The silver mines were an important part of Athens' increasing prosperity, but the stable and peaceful rule of the Peisistratids provided the fertile soil in which Athenian energy and enterprise could grow so dramatically into the springtime of Athens' greatness.

Chapter 8
Athenian Life and Art

Telling a story

We have seen again and again that much of the thinking of Archaic Greece was steeped in memories of the Heroic Age. By the middle of the eighth century a climax had been reached. It is typified by the Homeric epics, and by the vases of the Dipylon Master which towered above the tombs of aristocrats by Athens' Dipylon Gate. In a way, these works stand at the end of a line of development which could go no further. After them, poetry and painting were destined to find new paths; sculpture had scarcely begun. Homer had told tales to enthrall his hearers, and now artists began to try to do the same. Admittedly, human figures exist on the Dipylon vase mourning a corpse; but they are schematic shapes, with no individuality, and form part of the strong pattern which covers the vase above, below and on both sides of them.

Now, shaking off the animal friezes which they had copied from Corinth in the mid 600s, Athenian artists in the sixth century began the transformation from decoration to narrative on their vases. It was clearly impossible to tell an epic tale as Homer had, although Kleitias on his famous François Vase (c. 570 BC) perhaps achieved something of the sort. By depicting various scenes from the life of Achilles, from the wedding of his parents to the death of the hero, with other myths as well (there are 270 human and animal figures, and 121 names), he produced a collage effect which is both informative and decorative, and has a certain epic quality. Another method used by artists was the synoptic technique in which different stages of a story were all shown together in the same picture.

But artists preferred single events which could easily be portrayed in one picture. Herakles' labours fitted the bill to perfection, and this must be one reason why Herakles was perhaps the single most popular figure on Athenian vases before 510 BC. (He outnumbers Theseus, who became popular after the tyranny ended, by eight to one on surviving vases.) Another factor may have been the demands of the market where the vases were sold. Many surviving vases were found in southern Italy where the Dorian settlers would like to see vases depicting a Dorian hero. His twelve labours were not all equally appropriate, however, and for the 500 extant versions of Herakles fighting the Nemean lion, not one has survived of him cleansing the Augean Stables. It is not difficult to see why.

Like contemporary poets, who would often encapsulate the emotion of a moment in a short poem, artists excelled in capturing the high point of a dramatic event. And not always the physical climax, although these were beloved of black-figure artists, and most appropriate to their medium. Exekias, perhaps the finest black-figure artist, depicted Ajax planting the sword for his suicide, in a particularly quiet and poignant scene.

It should also be remembered that artists were attempting something quite different from Homer. Once the bard has spoken a line of verse, he must go on to the next: progression is all-important. The artist, on the other hand, must spread all his riches before us at once. Nevertheless, the same underlying principles can be seen: the archaic delight in contrast, pattern and balance – all are there in both media. A very popular theme on vases was Ajax and Achilles playing a board game, dressed in full armour, an incident unknown to us from any poem, and the version by Exekias (see fig. 11) shows all that is best about Archaic art.

Myth and the man in the street

The man in the street enjoyed a high exposure to art in sixth-century Athens. At the great festivals he attended performances of tragedy and comedy and listened to recitations of epic poetry. When he visited the Acropolis he saw an imposing temple, with beautiful statues around. Elsewhere, finely wrought objects of wood, bronze and marble enhanced his daily life. This was all part of his education, and through such art he learned about his city's past, and his rulers' aspirations for its future, for they were the principal patrons of the arts. Political ideas too must have been common coin, as the traditions and ideals of the *polis* were discussed. (The Greek word *politikos* means 'belonging to a *polis* – the Athenian citizen was 'political' by his very nature.) The foundations were being laid for the next century when Pericles, in a burst of patriotic fervour, could describe 'the whole city' as 'an education to Greece' (Thucydides 2.41).

The process was not new. Solon had used his poems to promote

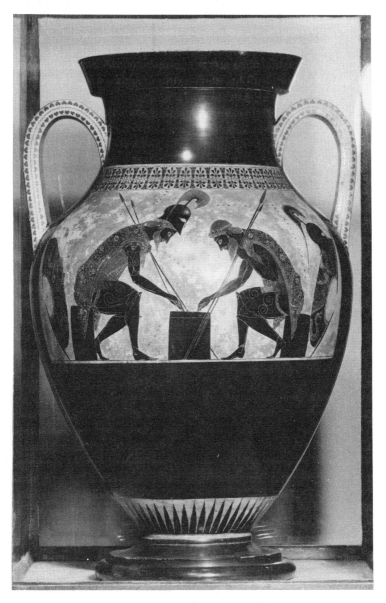

Fig. 11. Ajax and Achilles playing a board game, on a black-figure amphora painted and made by Exekias, 540-530 BC.

his political reforms back in 594 BC, and it has been suggested that Peisistratos was not above guiding the hands of artists in order to improve his own image. Herakles' popularity with vase painters during the tyranny has already been mentioned. After his laborious life the hero earned the right to join the immortals on Olympus, and his patron goddess Athene is seen leading him there and introducing him to Zeus. Although he appears in this scene both in a chariot and on foot before the 550s, it is only after that date that Athene first takes the reins herself. Did artists begin then to illustrate the Phye episode (p. 30), or did Peisistratos consciously imitate art in real life? As mentioned above, many examples survive of Ajax playing Achilles at a board game. It has been ingeniously suggested that this is a (light-hearted?) dig at the aristocrats who were caught napping when Peisistratos launched his third attack on Athens and won the battle of Pallene in 546 BC (see p. 33). And it is surely no accident that everyday scenes depicting fountain-houses become more common on vases after about 530 BC, sometimes featuring elaborate architecture – a reflection of Peisistratos' efforts to improve the water supply for the citizens of Athens (see chapter 7).

Herakles is also popular in the surviving sculptures from the Acropolis where he is found fighting Triton (twice), the Hydra, and being introduced to Olympus. It is an attractive theory that the Peisistratids themselves influenced the choice of subjects on these temple decorations, laying claim to a special relationship with Herakles, just as Peisistratos had taken Athene (patron goddess of Athens) and Herakles to himself as early as his second period of tyranny. Be that as it may, and such hypotheses must remain speculative – however seductive – we would not go amiss in seeing Herakles struggling, straining, heaving and in the end winning, as symbolic of the city herself during these competitive, but successful, years.

Noblesse oblige

As well as portraying gods and heroes in their multifarious adventures, vase painters enjoyed depicting scenes of everyday life. Such illustrations provide us with invaluable information – often the only evidence there is – for a wide range of activities. There are social occasions: we see Athenians feasting, drinking, making music, making love; there are religious occasions: funerals, wedding processions, and sacrifices; and there are sporting or athletic occasions: young men are painted in the gymnasium or wrestling-school and, inevitably, with horses. In fact on archaic red-figure vases there are more athletic scenes than any other in the everyday life genre. Industrial activity is less popular (except for pottery), but ploughing, sowing and olive-picking are regularly portrayed. In all of these, and in mythological pictures too, modern dress is worn, so there is an abundance of detailed evidence for how the well-dressed Athenian appeared in both war and peace.

Panathenaic vases were a specialised art-form, closely linked with athletic pursuits. As mentioned in chapter 7, they were given as prizes in the Great Panathenaia, and had a picture of Athene on one side and an event from the Games on the other. An inscription read '[I am] one of the prizes from Athens', and the vase was filled with precious olive oil. These *amphorae* (two-handled jars) were probably first made in 566/5 BC when the athletic contests were added to the Games, and in their size, shape and decoration they remained virtually unchanged into the fourth century. They were commissioned by the state, and were still painted in the old black-figure style long after it had had been superseded by red-figure.

Although young male aristocrats spent much time on athletics, music and military training, they also relaxed, and many vases show them reclining at *symposia* (drinking parties). Music and dancing girls might provide the entertainment, but the revellers would often amuse themselves by composing verses in competition with each other. Some of these improvisations (they were called *skolia*) are recorded, and the following anonymous verse reminds us of the value of true friendship, perhaps hard to find even in the close-knit circle of Athens' gilded youth:

> Oh that we could open the heart of every man, and read the thoughts within, then close it, and thus, undeceived, be sure of a friend.
>
> (Diehl 6)

Individual writing

The inscriptions on the François Vase by Kleitias have already been mentioned. From 570 BC onwards a significant minority of artists labelled the figures on their vases, often thus identifying for us the story being told. Sometimes the painter's spelling is faulty; sometimes nonsense letters are used, apparently for decorative effect; and sometimes the letters run backwards, as in some stone inscriptions of this period.

At the same time, artists began to sign their work: Sophilos is the first complete name to have survived (c. 580-570 BC). We also read the names of potters on vases and, it is believed, of studio-owners. Nevertheless, although over 100 names of potters and painters are known from vases produced in Athens before the Persian Wars, it is by their individual styles that very many more painters have been identified.

Another interesting group of inscriptions consists of the word *kalos* ('handsome, beautiful') joined to the name of a contemporary Athenian youth, who usually has no connection with the picture on the vase. Sometimes he can be identified, and so provide evidence for the date of the vase. The precise significance of these *kalos* inscriptions is unclear; but they were probably intended as a compliment to a young nobleman who was well known for his good looks, and they are unlikely to imply any intimacy on the part of the painter.

Incidentally, such writing on vases presumably intended for general circulation provides evidence for the steady spread of literacy during this period. By the fifth century the average male Athenian citizen could read and write, if only at a fairly basic level, and this literacy helped to speed some of the changes taking place at this time, not only in Athens but in the Greek world as a whole.

The signing of names on vases is also typical of the individualism which marks the sixth century. Potters and painters wished to be remembered for their work, as indeed had the poets of the previous century. We ascribe the *Iliad* and the *Odyssey* to Homer, but it may well be that they were not composed by the same man. At any rate they were the culmination of a long tradition of oral poetry, anonymous by its very nature, as each bard would make his own improvements or alterations to the stories as he recited them – every performance being, in a way, a new poem. (The nearest we ever get to a personal touch in the *Odyssey* is in line 1: 'Tell me, O Muse, of the resourceful man who...'). Then, with the coming of writing the poems were written down, and so the written version became the standard one and the poems were frozen, as it were, and their development ceased. We see the same process in the ballads of the Scottish Borders, all of them anonymous, which Sir Walter Scott collected, touched up and published, thus preserving them, and making them available to a wider public.

This is a sign of the change from an oral to a literate tradition. Poetry changed from epic, partly with the invention of writing, and partly as a reaction against Homer. The sheer excellence of his works must have daunted the more thoughtful and talented of the poets who came after, and made them look for different ways of expressing themselves. The poets of the seventh and sixth centuries are called lyric and elegaic poets, and their poems tend to be shorter and more personal, often telling the reader more about the poet himself than re-telling the age-old myths. (Only the Homeric Hymns kept the Homeric tradition alive in the sixth and fifth centuries. These were anonymous preludes composed in honour of a god: the Hymn to Demeter, for example, told the foundation myth of the Eleusinian Mysteries.)

This individualism in art was matched by a similar trend in society. Previously, society consisted of the aristocracy and the rabble, which is virtually what we see in Homer's poems. But during the seventh century individuals outside the aristocracy became more important, with consequent social and political change. Tyrannies rose and fell, aristocrats continued to struggle with each other, but in the developing *polis* the citizen found a voice of his own. And not only was he a man with his own rights as an individual, but he was also aware of the benefits of submerging these rights in order to fight alongside his fellow-citizens for the common good. He did not insist on fighting in single combat, as his aristocratic masters had done in the past. Like the oarsman in an eight, he knew that the *polis* which gave him his raison d'être would be best defended by fighting in the hoplite team. There is a nice tension here: citizenship, with its rewards and responsibilities, was being born.

Man was now entering a new phase in his social development: already he was light years away from the monarchies of Mycenean Greece, the authoritarian empire of the Great King, or the bureaucracy of Egypt. Tentatively, like someone seeing or walking for the first time, he was stepping into a new world. The experience was heady, but he knew what he was doing. The lyric poet Phokylides of Miletos caught the feeling well in a brief fragment (note the 'signature' in the opening):

Phokylides also says this: a small, well-organised city which is built on a rock, is better than senseless Nineveh.

(Diehl 4)

Foreign inspiration

The most striking aspect of the signatures on Athenian vases of this period is the high proportion of foreign names: for example *Lydos* ('the Lydian'), *Sikelos* ('the Sicilian'), *Skuthes* ('the Scythian') and *Thrax* ('the Thracian'). These are unlikely to refer to the owner's nationality, but they may denote his place of origin, or perhaps they were used as nicknames by Athenians who could not easily get their tongues round foreign names. Others actually are foreign names, like *Amasis*, for instance, an Egyptian name with which Exekias actually labelled a negro on one of his vases. A third group of names seems to refer to personal characteristics, like *Smikros* ('tiny'). Many of these would be first- or second-generation immigrants, and either slaves or *metics* (resident aliens without the full rights of citizens).

The same is true of sculptors. Out of a much smaller total of names (some two dozen in Athens), there are Gorgias of Sparta, Euenor of Ephesos, Bion of Miletos, Aristion of Paros and Archermos (and his sons) of Chios – all clearly foreigners; while *Philergos* ('hard-working') and *Phaidimos* ('brilliant') were not too diffident to advertise themselves on their creations.

The reason for this influx of foreigners to Athens is not hard to find. From the middle of the sixth century onwards, Greeks began to leave Ionia and move to the islands or the Greek mainland. First, there was the threat of Lydia, which had conquered many of the *poleis* and exacted tribute from as early as 600 BC. Then, when Cyrus the Great had defeated King Croesus of Lydia in 546 BC and taken his capital Sardis, Persian rule over the continent stopped only at the Aegean Sea. Bias of Priene, one of the Seven Sages, even recommended that the Ionians should emigrate en masse and colonise Sardinia (Hdt. 1.170), but they shrank from so radical a step. As these Ionian Greeks travelled west, many would come to Athens which, as a wealthy and flourishing centre, had a lot to offer the incomer, including plenty of commissions, both public and private, for the artist. As soon as Athens began to flower as an artistic centre, it became a Mecca for every aspiring artist. The progression was inevitable.

So far, literature has scarcely been mentioned, and it is perhaps surprising that, apart from Solon, no Athenian writer of any importance is known from the sixth century. One literary art-form which did flourish at this time was the drinking song or *skolion*, mentioned above (p. 71) However, the sons of Peisistratos, holding high court in the 520s BC, drew into their orbit two of the greatest living lyric poets: Simonides of Keos and Anakreon of Teos, the latter an exile from the court of Polykrates of Samos after the Persians took over the island. Simonides wrote hymns and odes for public performance, while Anakreon entertained his patrons with witty epigrams and playful lyrics (see chapter 9).

Eastern influence is obvious in earlier phases of Greek art. One era is even named the Orientalising Period by art historians, and it seems almost certain that the inspiration for monumental architecture and free-standing stone statues (*kouroi*) came from Egypt. In the period after Solon's reforms the influence of immigrant Corinthian potters and painters can be seen in the shapes and decoration of Athenian vases (see chapter 5) – the result of Solon's encouragement to foreign craftsmen to settle in Athens with their families. Despite the number of foreign signatures, however, no particular outside influence can be detected on black-figure and red-figure vases after 550 BC. In sculpture, on the other hand, it is possible to detect an East Greek touch in the carving here and there. Sculptors were more mobile than potters – they followed the commissions, and would take with them the skills and styles learned in their homeland.

By about 530 BC, however, mainland Greek art was going its own way, and any ideas that came from abroad were quickly adapted by Greek artists to their own purposes. Nowhere was this more true than at Athens. A century later Pericles was to attract all the best sculptors and stonemasons in Greece to effect his building programme. Under the Peisistratids the city was growing rapidly, welcoming any foreign talent which arrived, and providing an artistic melting-pot where new and ever higher standards of excellence were being set.

Perpetuum mobile

Thanks to the Persian sack of the Acropolis in 480 BC (see p. 55), more Archaic sculpture has survived from Athens than from anywhere else, and so our view of sixth-century Greek sculpture is dominated by Athenian remains. Nevertheless, whatever was being produced elsewhere, few other *poleis* could have given their citizens more to admire and discuss than Athens did.

In any Archaic *polis* the temple towered above the surrounding buildings, which were never more than two storeys high, and in Athens the temple to Athene Polias (see p. 55) already stood high on the

Acropolis, clear against the deep blue sky. Here the Athenian making an offering, attending a sacrifice, or watching the Panathenaic procession, had seen sculptors make the transition from decoration to narrative on pediments and metopes. Unfortunately, only separate fragments remain of the two sets of pedimental sculptures, and there is disagreement on how they might have fitted into the pediments. The earlier group, made of limestone, includes several wild animals (lions and bulls), a rather jolly snake-like creature with three human heads and shoulders named Bluebeard after the traces of paint remaining on it, and, to celebrate the triumph of civilisation, Herakles fighting Triton.

The later (520 BC) marbles which are thought to have replaced them are even more fragmentary, but there was a Gigantomachy (Battle of Gods and Giants) which shows considerable advances on the limestone groups. Here, human figures twist and turn with new confidence and the sculptor planted a towering Athene with her snaky aegis in the high centre of the awkward triangular shape of the pediment, with dying or falling giants, of similar scale, filling the corners. Such figures, brightly painted in their shining marble setting (and presumably commissioned by the state, i.e. the Peisistratids), must have astonished and delighted the Athenians who gazed on them in the last years of the tyrants' reign.

Also standing on the Acropolis were many votive offerings, sometimes just inscribed slabs, but often free-standing marble statues of naked young men (*kouroi*) or young women (*korai*) carved in brightly painted clothes. One memorable statue which has survived is the Rampin Horseman, which seems to have been one of a pair, and so may just possibly have been a dedication by the two sons of Peisistratos. There would also be bronze statues, but only a handful of bronzes have survived from antiquity – the rest, alas, having been melted down and put to other uses. And somewhere among all these stood that most endearing of Archaic sculptures, the Calf-bearer, the calf's gentle face reminding us that Athens, for all its cosmopolitan sophistication, had its roots in the soil.

The series of *kouroi* are the most prominent of the statues of this century. Standing sentinel over graves, or as dedications in sanctuaries, they proclaimed the devotion to the gods, or to their forebears, of the wealthy individuals who commissioned them, and also provided a way of keeping up with the aristocratic Joneses. They too underwent a steady transformation during the sixth century.

The early versions, while clearly symbolising young men (see fig. 4), are unlike the human figure in so many ways (the stiff, unnatural pose, the patterned muscles and hair, the lingering impression of the rectangular block of stone they are carved from) that one feels the sculptor only used the human body as a model in the most rudimentary way. These figures are schematic, not lifelike, although they have a haunting beauty and stillness, sometimes even a latent energy, of their own.

But as the century progressed, sculptors made the features of their *kouroi* gradually more lifelike, apparently moving by trial and error towards a more effective image of the ideal youth – although not necessarily aiming for total realism. Then the day came when a passer-by realised with a shock that an unusually imaginative sculptor had carved a figure which, in a twilit graveyard perhaps, might be mistaken for a real person (see fig. 6). Once that point had been reached, there was no turning back. Soon afterwards sculptors saw how awkwardly the *kouros* stood: the pose was altered, and a new era began in which art attempted truly to represent nature.

This chapter is not intended to be a survey of Archaic Greek art, even for the fifty or so years of Peisistratid influence or rule in Athens. But by touching on some of the developments taking place in all the arts at this time, it is hoped that some impression will be given of the exciting innovations which Athens experienced during the tyranny.

Any time he wanted, the Athenian could stroll through the Kerameikos (Potters' Quarter) between the Agora and the Dipylon Gate and watch the artists at work, or admire the rows of colourful vases already fired. Pottery was big business in Athens, although we should not entertain visions based on modern industry. A limited number of hard workers, perhaps a few hundred at most, produced vases which were sold all over the world. Athenians even designed specific pots for particular markets: for example, they developed a special Etruscan shape for sale in Etruria. A coveted commission, on offer every four years, must have been to make the Panathenaic prize vases which, in the early fourth century BC, amounted to well over a thousand for a single Games.

Hesiod had commented two centuries earlier on how 'neighbour competes with neighbour as he pursues wealth...potter is angry with potter, and craftsman with craftsman' (*Works and Days* 25-6). But the rivalry could also be friendly. Detective work on the vases produced by the Pioneer Group, active from about 520 BC, reveals artists greeting each other in inscriptions, and even boasting of their prowess. On a vase depicting three revellers, signed by Euthymides, appear the words 'as never Euphronios', meaning 'Euphronios never painted as well as this' (see fig. 12).

Fig. 12. Three revellers on an Attic red-figure belly amphora signed by Euthymides (about 510 BC). One of the earliest examples of figures drawn in three-quarter view, a treatment which hints at three-dimensional reality on a two-dimensional surface.

What Euthymides was especially proud of on this vase was his rendering of anatomy, and this was made possible by the change from black-figure to red-figure around 530 BC. This development, startling at first, yet obvious once it was thought of, revolutionised the depiction of the human body on vases by giving scope for much greater subtlety; and it is likely that experiments in drawing like those of Euthymides influenced contemporary sculptors. Now for the first time painters show men in three-quarter view, rather than fixing a profile head on a frontal body with profile legs. It is a happy thought that Peisistratos must have seen the new red-figure designs shortly before his death, and taken comfort in the knowledge that there were now resident in Athens enough talented artists to ensure that Athenian red-figure vases would dominate world markets as black-figure had.

Who were these artists? Many of them were foreigners, as we have seen, and even the native Athenians would be of lowly social status. Virtually none of the signatures on vases is from the same social class as the *kalos* names. Unlike the poet, who was regarded as a man directly inspired by the gods, painters, potters and sculptors were treated as craftsmen who used their skills to produce objects for sale, either for personal or religious use. As far as we know, neither marble nor bronze statues stood inside private houses to decorate them; vases were for storing or carrying something, not for decoration alone, or putting flowers in. While Anakreon and Simonides might be fêted in the tyrants' court, even a superb potter and painter like Exekias remained an artisan. Nevertheless, some might make a good living – two potters were wealthy enough to dedicate a bronze statue on the Acropolis – and sculptors became famous in the following century. But there was never a Muse of painting or sculpture, and there are no references to vase painting in the Greek literature which has survived.

Such was the diverse and thriving city over which the tyrants presided. The ordinary Athenian might admire or envy the extravagant lifestyle of the aristocracy, watching the young men as they raced their horses and ran and wrestled in the games, or avoiding them as they revelled drunkenly through the streets at night after their *symposia*. But from the lofty Acropolis to the lowly Kerameikos there was an abundance of works of art to delight his eyes. He could also wander through the graveyards where the wealthy honoured their dead with imposing marble *kouroi* or with solemn gravestones carved in fine relief. And the city's growing wealth became tangible for him when he handled the solid little 'owls' of Athens, minted from her native silver.

Chapter 9
The Final Years

Palaces and pleasures

Peisistratos died in 528/7 BC. [Aristotle] writes:

> When Peisistratos died, his sons took over the rule and carried on the government in the same way...Hipparchos and Hippias were in charge of affairs because of their reputation and their age. Hippias, who was the elder of the two and had a natural interest in politics as well as being a man of good sense, took charge of the rule. Hipparchos was childish, amorous and a lover of the arts – he was the one who had brought the circle of Anakreon and Simonides and the other poets to Athens. Thessalos was much younger, and enjoyed a bold and insolent lifestyle...
> (*Constitution of Athens* 17.3 and 18.1-2)

[Aristotle] then goes on to describe the murder of Hipparchos in 514 BC and the end of the reign four years later. Before that, however, Hippias and Hipparchos enjoyed over a decade of comparatively trouble-free rule. These must have been good years for Athens, when the seeds which Peisistratos had planted and nurtured continued to bear fruit. The honeymoon period of appeasement with rival families, which was revealed by the archon list found in the Agora, has already been discussed. The tyrants' sons now had the resources to indulge their fancies, and Athens continued to grow.

Now she was savouring the kind of prosperity which Corinth had enjoyed around 600 BC when, in the court of the tyrant Periander, the poet Arion of Lesbos had flourished, inventing the dithyramb – an ode in praise of Dionysos for choral singing; when Corinthian vases had captured and held the markets for half a century, and when Corinth had built one of the first Doric temples. Another spur to the ambitions of the sons of Peisistratos must have been the building achievements of Polykrates, tyrant of Samos, only recently done to death by a Persian satrap after being lured away from the safety of his island.

It was from Samos that Hipparchos rescued the lyric poet Anakreon of Teos, who entertained the literati of Athens with the vivid imagery of his poems about love and life.

> The God of Love has hammered me again, like a blacksmith with his huge axe, and plunged me into a wintry torrent.
>
> (*Poetae Melici Graeci* 413)

Anakreon's verses glitter, but there is also an objectivity about some of them, and a self-conscious delight in his own cleverness. We can picture the luxury of Hipparchos' court, but also perhaps its fragility.

> Come, boy – bring me a flagon
> that I may drink it in one large gulp.
> Pour out ten measures of water to five of wine,
> so that I may play the Bacchante –
> within limits.
>
> (*Poetae Melici Graeci* 356)

Nevertheless, this is the counterpart in verse to the merry scenes on vase paintings of *symposia*, with tipsy aristocrats enjoying the delights of flute girls and pretty boys; and in fact Anakreon is named as the lyre-player on three early red-figure vases depicting *symposia*. Legend said that he died at the ripe old age of 85, choked by a grape pip.

Anakreon was not the only poet at court. Hipparchos too felt inspired to try his hand, and turned out moral maxims in verse, such as

> Hipparchos says: do not think crooked thoughts

and

> Hipparchos says: do not deceive a friend.

(The former seems to be a pun, for the word meaning 'crooked thoughts' is *skolia*, the plural of *skolion*.) He had these gems inscribed on herms, which were usually stone pillars topped by the head of Hermes (god of trade and travellers), with an erect phallos lower down, and set them up midway between the Altar of the Twelve Gods in Athens (dedicated by Hippias' son Peisistratos in 522/1) and various districts in Attica.

This quasi-religious flavour was no doubt encouraged by Onomakritos, a collector of oracles, and one of Hipparchos' circle, until he was discovered forging some oracles and banished from

Athens. He reappears nearly forty years on at the court of King Xerxes of Persia in Susa where, in cahoots with the exiled Peisistratidai, he is again to be found doctoring the sacred texts in an attempt to persuade the Great King to invade Greece (Herodotus 7.6). There was, of course, political purpose in the collecting and control of oracles, and Peisistratos himself had been a past master in the exploitation of religion, even enjoying the nickname 'Bakis' – a name commonly given to soothsayers.

Such activities, however, would have little effect on the average Athenian. What he saw were startling new marble pediments on the temple of Athene Polias on the Acropolis, a rash of new dedications in the sanctuary around it, and the start of a colossal new temple to Olympian Zeus to the south-east of the citadel – the Peisistratids' answer to Polykrates' temple to Hera on Samos, built ten years before. He probably also began to hear the works of Homer recited every four years at the Great Panathenaia. So while Hipparchos and his cultured friends enjoyed the rewards of tyranny, the man in the street, as he watched Athens continue to prosper, had nothing to complain of.

Straws in the wind

Nevertheless, during this period some clouds began to form on the horizon. In 520 BC the formidable Kleomenes had become king of Sparta, and a year later he was 'in the neighbourhood with an army', as Herodotus mysteriously puts it, when the men of Plataia, a border town on the Theban side of Mount Kithairon, asked him for help against the Thebans who were pressing them hard. With masterly diplomacy he advised them to turn to Athens instead; this they did, and an alliance was formed. Thus at a stroke Kleomenes avoided, without loss of face, a potentially awkward involvement for Sparta far to the north in central Greece, and at the same time he effectively ended Athenian friendship with Thebes. Soon afterwards, Athens helped Plataia fight a battle against Thebes and, in winning, made enemies of the Thebans for years to come (Herodotus 6.108).

In about 517 BC the Spartans deposed Lygdamis of Naxos, and a Peisistratid ally in mid-Aegean was lost. If there were any Athenian nobles whose children were still being held hostage on Naxos, they would now be emboldened to oppose the tyrants more openly. It is not clear when the Peisistratids' murder of Kimon, the Philaid with the wonderful stable, became generally known, or even suspected. But awareness of such a nervous and clumsy action can only have fuelled aristocratic determination to oust them. If the tyrants were not actually guilty, the fact that they were suspected points to their increasing unpopularity.

In 514 BC the ominous shadow of Persia fell across Europe. King Darius mounted an expedition against the Scythian tribes north of the Danube, leaving his Ionian forces behind to guard the bridge. Although given the chance to maroon him in the Scythian wilderness, the tyrants of the Ionian *poleis*, who knew too well which side their bread was buttered, stood firm for the Great King, to whom they owed their authority. The expedition failed, but the writing was on the wall. A Persian force was left in Europe to subdue the north coast of the Aegean as far as the borders of Macedonia, so Peisistratid links with the mines by Mount Pangaion, presumably still an important source of revenue, would now be severed. Sigeion was already in Persian territory.

The Ionian poet Xenophanes, writing some years earlier, struck the chord which was to echo down several generations of Greeks. In the imaginary safety of a *symposion* (he had settled in the west), he asks the usual questions which Homeric heroes ask of each other, but adds a sting in the tail:

> Thus you should speak by the fire in the winter season,
> as you lie on a soft couch, full of food,
> drinking sweet wine, and chewing chick peas:
> 'Who are you? Where do you come from? Who were your
> family and parents?
> How old were you when the Persians came?'

To a thoughtful tyrant, the future must have begun to look less rosy by 514 BC: most of the tyrants now left in the Greek world were in Ionia and propped up by Persia. Which way could Hippias turn if the going became rough? Perhaps his mind was concentrated by the death of his brother.

The gathering storm

It was in the excited bustle that preceded the procession of the Great Panathenaia in 514 BC that Hipparchos was assassinated. He had taken a fancy to a beautiful youth called Harmodios who already had a male lover named Aristogeiton. When Hipparchos' advances were rebuffed, he insulted the boy and his family by inviting his sister to take part in a ritual procession, and then sending her home on the day as unsuitable. This incensed both Harmodios and Aristogeiton, who was already afraid that he might lose the boy to the tyrant should Hipparchos decide to pull rank. They therefore plotted together with others to murder both Hippias and Hipparchos, and planned to do it on the day of the Great Panathenaia.

When the day came, they noticed one of the conspirators talking to Hippias in a friendly manner and assumed that their plot was betrayed. Wishing to achieve something worthwhile before they were caught, they rushed at Hipparchos and cut him down. Harmodios was killed on the spot by the bodyguard, and Aristogeiton was tortured to death in an attempt to find the names of the other conspirators.

Herodotus recounts the incident very briefly, without giving any motive for the deed (5.55-6). [Aristotle] gives a fuller account, but Thucydides devotes several pages to the affair, including the interesting comments that Hippias was 'a man whom anyone could easily approach' (6.57.2), and that the conspirators hoped others would join in the attempt to set Athens free, even though they were not part of the plot. In fact nobody did and it took a Spartan army, and a stroke of bad luck, to dislodge Hippias in the end.

But Thucydides' main aim seems to be to correct beliefs about these events which were held in Athens at the time he was writing (about 415 BC). In particular, he goes to considerable lengths to prove that Hippias, not Hipparchos, was tyrant at the time; that the murder was largely the result of a personal quarrel; and that the death of Hipparchos did not bring an end to tyranny. Neither [Aristotle] nor Herodotus disagrees with any of these statements, and it must be assumed that other versions were current in the late fifth century, perhaps derived from one or other of the Atthidographers (see p. 8).

One source of error must have been the *skolion* which was heard soon after, celebrating the great deed:

> Their glory shall live on earth for ever –
> Harmodios and Aristogeiton most dear –
> Since they killed the tyrant
> And gave fair laws to Athens
>
> (*Poetae Melici Graeci* 896)

Such a song, composed at a *symposion*, but no doubt soon enjoying a wider audience, shows an indifference to truth typical of verses inspired by local patriotism. In the years that followed it became easy for Athenians to play down the importance of Alkmeonid and Spartan influence, and their own apathy, and to exaggerate the role of the two lovers as freedom-fighters. They had in fact achieved nothing, except to make Hippias afraid, but their murder of Hipparchos soon became the official version of the end of the tyranny. They received sacrifices and libations, and their statues were set up in the Agora. It was all a great democratic myth.

At any rate, Herodotus, [Aristotle] and Thucydides all agree in saying that after Hipparchos' death the tyranny took a decisive turn for the worse.

> After this the tyranny became harsher for the Athenians and Hippias, more fearful now, had many citizens executed, and at the same time began to look abroad for a place of refuge in case there was a revolution. Certainly it was after this that Hippias, although he was an Athenian, gave his daughter Archedike to a Lampsakene, Aiantides, the son of Hippoklos the tyrant of Lampsakos, because he knew that they had great influence with King Darius of Persia.
>
> (THUCYDIDES 6.59.2-3)

By now it must be assumed that many aristocrats were back in exile again, working against the Peisistratids. Apart from the shadowy Kedon, mentioned by [Aristotle] (20.5) as having 'attacked the tyrants' at an unspecified time, the first invasion came in 513 BC when they fortified Leipsydrion, at the foot of Mount Parnes in the northern hill-country of Attica. Although some support came from the city, Hippias proved too strong for them, and this *skolion*, written to commemorate the disaster, underlines the essentially aristocratic nature of the attempt:

> Alas, Leipsydrion, betrayer of comrades,
> What men you destroyed –
> Good fighters and nobly born –
> Who showed on that day what stuff they were made of.
>
> (quoted in *Constitution of Athens* 19.3)

Kleisthenes the Alkmeonid, who seems to have been blessed with an abundant supply of his family's guile and opportunism, now turned to less direct methods. He was based at Delphi, where the great temple had been accidentally burnt down in 548 BC.

> The Alkmeonidai, doing everything they could to thwart the Peisistratidai, won the contract to build the temple at Delphi...They were men of means, and their family had

been distinguished from of old, and the temple they built
was finer than the one which had been planned in several
respects; in particular, they made the façade of Parian
marble, whereas the plan had been for the whole temple to
be made of limestone.

(HERODOTUS 5.62)

The timing of this feat (which the archaeological evidence seems
to confirm) is not clear. Herodotus puts it after the defeat at
Leipsydrion, but the building of the temple probably began earlier.
Such a grandiose public gesture was typical of the Alkmeonidai: it
would win them international prestige, and the Delphic priesthood
would surely now be eating out of their hands. Herodotus continues:

According to the Athenians these men, during their stay at
Delphi, bribed the Priestess to tell any Spartans who came
to consult the oracle, whether on private or public business,
that they ought to liberate Athens.

(HERODOTUS 5.63)

Bribery may hardly have been necessary, after the marble façade
was in place, and this part of the story could be an anti-Alkmeonid
tradition picked up by Herodotus. At any rate, the cultivation of the
unsuspecting Spartans soon bore fruit.

Herodotus says later that the Peisistratidai were good friends of
the Spartans, but that 'divine commands took precedence over human
ties.'(5.63) However, there were probably other reasons for the
Spartans agreeing to 'liberate' Athens and instal a pro-Spartan
oligarchy. Herodotus, Thucydides and [Aristotle] all say that Sparta
had a policy of unseating tyrants; and in the case of Athens we can see
motives enough in Peisistratid friendship with Argos, an inveterate
enemy of Sparta, in their strong connections with Thessaly, a powerful
northern state, and also in Hippias' recent marriage alliance with
Hippoklos, the pro-Persian tyrant of Lampsakos.

In about 512 BC a sea-borne invasion force arrived at Phaleron,
commanded by the Spartan Anchimolios. The Peisistratidai, who
'knew of their plans in advance' (Herodotus 5.63.3), had sent to
Thessaly for help, and the thousand cavalry which came south to
Athens (a useful legacy of Peisistratos' northern alliances), proved
enough to rout the invaders, killing their leader.

Hippias could breathe again; but not for long. Spartan pride was
now at stake. The noose was tightening.

The last curtain

The end, when it came, was something of an anti-climax. Hippias had begun to build a fort on the rock of Mounychia, west of the bay of Phaleron, and overlooking the natural harbour where the great port of Piraeus was to be constructed a generation later. It would be a good place to defend in a crisis, or perhaps a jumping-off point for flight overseas. But it was too late. King Kleomenes himself arrived by land with a larger army in 510 BC.

> When the Spartans advanced into Attica, the Thessalian cavalry engaged them first but were soon routed, with the loss of over forty men. The survivors went straight back to Thessaly. Kleomenes arrived at Athens and with the help of those Athenians who wanted to be free, besieged the tyrants, who were walled up on the Acropolis. The Spartans would have had little chance of capturing the Peisistratids. They had not intended to undertake a siege and the Peisistratids had plenty of food and drink, so the Spartans would probably have gone back home after besieging them for a few days. But as it was, something happened which proved to be a stroke of luck for the Spartans, but a disaster for their enemies: as they were being smuggled out of the country, the children of the Peisistratids were captured. This threw all their plans into confusion and, in order to save their children, they came to terms with the Athenians and agreed to leave Attica within five days. Afterwards, they withdrew to Sigeion on the Skamander.
>
> (HERODOTUS 5.64-5)

The Peisistratidai moved on easily to another city after leaving Athens. In fact Sigeion happened to be a personal possession of the family, but the old Homeric custom of *xenia* (see p. 34) made it natural for an exiled nobleman to go to friends elsewhere and plot his return with their help. Peisistratos had done it, the Alkmeonidai had now done it; probably Hippias left Attica confident that he would soon return, albeit with foreign aid. His primary concern was, after all, the supremacy of his family, and he would never have seen it as treachery to attack his own city to regain control of it. But the new citizens of the *poleis* were about to start transforming the old competitive code. Whereas personal glory at any cost was the aim in the age of heroes, now glory could be won if you died fighting for your own city. The state was beginning to replace the family as the focal point of a citizen's loyalty. Cooperation was taking the place of competition. Exceptional individuals like Themistokles and Alkibiades would still flee abroad and find refuge: they, and others like them, assumed they could continue under the old system. But the *polis* now demanded, and in most cases received, the loyalty of its citizens; and they took their revenge on the aristocrats who refused to play by the new rules.

The popularity of the tyranny is also remarkable, or perhaps the apathy of the Athenians. There was never a popular uprising against the Peisistratids. Despite Herodotus' (possibly anachronistic) remark about 'those Athenians who wanted to be free', the Spartans seem not to have expected much local help. The beginning and end of tyranny in Athens was marked by the presence of foreign troops. Hippias during his last years, and other tyrants elsewhere, gave tyranny its bad name, but Peisistratos' reign soon came to be seen as a Golden Age – and we can understand why.

It is not easy to get close to the personalities of Peisistratos and his sons, and there is the added problem of knowing which member of the family should be credited with many of the tyranny's achievements. The father had acquired impressive connections for himself before we first meet him in middle age, but his statesmanship and ability to cope with his rivals thereafter speak for themselves. Simonides is said to have compared him to a Siren, perhaps another way of describing an iron hand in a velvet glove. Hippias seems to have ruled capably enough before the death of Hipparchos, and his family's contributions to the arts deserve praise. He may have been less of a statesman than his father, but he was overtaken by events partly beyond his control: the advance of Persia and Sparta's military might proved too strong a combination, especially with Kleisthenes' machinations added to the mix.

The departure of Hippias also sees the beginning of the end of useful interchange of ideas between east and west. The military confrontation between Greece and Persia, which dominates the next century, saw to that. Herodotus' enquiring nature, typical of an Ionian, is part of the attractiveness of his work, and this openness is missing from later history, which is the history of the *polis*. Indeed Herodotus is criticised by Plutarch for his open-mindedness, and called a 'barbarian-lover'.

Epilogue

Twenty years later, in 490 BC, Hippias returned to Attica, and landed at Marathon with a Persian army. An old man now, it was his last chance of being reinstated as tyrant of Athens. Herodotus celebrates his last visit to Attica with the following anecdote:

> Hippias was leading the Persians to Marathon, and on the previous night he had dreamed that he was sleeping with his mother. As a result of this dream he believed that he would return to Athens, become ruler again, and die an old man in his own country...While he was busy showing the invaders where to go, he happened to sneeze and cough more violently than usual, and as he was a fairly old man, and most of his teeth were loose, he coughed one of them right out of his mouth. It fell on to the sand, and despite all his efforts, he was unable to find it, so he said with a groan to the bystanders: 'This land is not ours, and we shall never be able to conquer it. My tooth now owns whatever share I ever had in it.'
>
> (HERODOTUS 6.107)

Did he expect an unopposed march to Athens, supporters joining them on the way, and an easy victory near the city, just as in 546 BC? If so, he was sadly disappointed; for since Kleisthenes the Alkmeonid had given Athens democracy in 507 BC, she had become a new creation. And the irony was that it was Hippias and his father who made democracy possible.

Thucydides describes the tyrants as men who ruled with 'high principles and practical intelligence' (6.54.5), praise he grants to only a few men in his history. By reining in the warring nobility, Peisistratos set the city free to thrive and prosper. As it became gradually more unified under his strong central authority, the power of the local landlords withered away. He provided peace at home and markets abroad for the economy to flourish. The patronage of the tyrants encouraged the flowering of every art, and glorified the city in the process. The competitive impulse was channelled into peaceful pursuits; and the Peisistratids' genial control of affairs gave room for intellectual speculation and artistic experiment which led to new concepts of freedom.

In a way, Hippias' hopes were not unrealistic: the Athenian victory at Marathon seemed a miracle to Greeks at the time. But the world had changed. The age of heroes was over, and a new age had dawned.

Suggestions for Further Study

1. Consider the various modern theories for the rise of tyranny: how convincing are they? What is the evidence for them? Andrewes (*Greek Society* p. 63) thinks he may have got things 'back to front' with his hoplite theory: what do you think? Read what Aristotle says about tyranny: how convincing are his theories? (See Andrewes, *The Greek Tyrants* for references).

2. Compare the tyranny in Athens with tyrannies elsewhere. Why did tyranny come late to Athens? (Reading: Jeffery, and Andrewes, *The Greek Tyrants*).

3. How good are Solon's poems as evidence for his reforms?

4. Herodotus the historian. Compare the different types of evidence he used, discussing examples of each. What are their relative merits? Was Herodotus aware of these? Consider the sources for his account of the tyranny in Athens: what might they have been? Can you discern any trace of bias?

5. Herodotus and Thucydides. Find out what Thucydides says about Herodotus (directly and by implication). Is he fair? Compare the stated aims of both historians. Which of the two methods have historians tended to follow since? Why? Has this been good or bad for the development of history?

6. Find out more about what happened at the major festivals in Athens. What sort of evidence do we have for them? What are the modern equivalents of such events? Compare the Parthenon frieze with what we know of the Great Panathenaia: what differences/similarities are there?

7. Find out the differences between Ionic and Doric architecture, with examples of each. Consider the purpose of the buildings of the

Peisistratidai: can you discern any development from father to sons?

8. Investigate further the theories about Peisistratid propaganda in the art of this period. How convincing are they?

9. Read Pindar's 7th *Pythian Ode*, in honour of the Alkmeonid Megakles (grandson of the Megakles who won the Contest of the Suitors). This Megakles whom Pindar is praising was ostracised (banished for ten years) shortly before his victory. Admire the poet's skill!

10. Read as much poetry of this period as possible, and look at the works of art which have survived. Try to imagine what it must have felt like to be an Athenian aristocrat, a 'man in the street', a woman, an artist, and so on.

Suggestions for Further Reading

Ancient evidence

The Penguin Classics series has translations of Homer, Herodotus, Plutarch's *Life of Solon* (in *The Rise and Fall of Athens*), Aristotle's *Politics* and *The Athenian Constitution* (with some helpful notes). Richmond Lattimore's *Greek Lyrics* (Chicago, 1960 2nd ed.) is a short but useful selection, including translations of poems by Solon, Anakreon, Simonides, Phokylides and Xenophanes, and some *skolia*. My numbering of Solon's poems is from M.L. West's *Iambi et Elegi Graeci* (Oxford, 1971), and of the other poems either from D.L. Page's *Poetae Melici Graeci* (Oxford, 1962) or E. Diehl's *Anthologia Lyrica Graeca* (Leipzig). These last three volumes have Greek texts only, as has *A Selection of Greek Historical Inscriptions* by R. Meiggs and D.M. Lewis (Oxford, 1969).

Modern works

Andrewes A., *The Greek Tyrants* (Hutchinson, 1956). A full account of the rise and fall of all the tyrants. Propounds the theory that the development of the hoplite army was a major factor in the rise of tyranny.

Andrewes, A., *Greek Society* (Penguin, 1971). Good introduction to social and political institutions.

Boardman, J., *Athenian Black Figure Vases* (1974), *Athenian Red Figure Vases: The Archaic Period* (Thames and Hudson, 1975) and *Greek Sculpture: The Archaic Period* (Thames and Hudson, 1978) are all invaluable handbooks with a wealth of illustrations.

Boersma, J.S., *Athenian Building Policy 561/0–405/4 BC* (Groningen, 1970). A very detailed analysis of the buildings of this period and their purpose.

Bowra, C.M., *Greek Lyric Poetry* (Oxford, 1936). Includes chapters on Anakreon, Simonides, and the *skolia*.

Burn, A.R., *The Lyric Age of Greece* (Arnold, 1960). An excellent and detailed survey of every aspect of this period.

Burn, A.R., *The Pelican History of Greece* (Penguin, 1966). A lively introduction for the general reader.

The Cambridge Ancient History (2nd edition) Vol III Part 3 has two chapters (by A. Andrewes) on the period covered by this book, with a section on the chronological problems, and a full bibliography.

Forrest, W.G., *The Emergence of Greek Democracy* (Weidenfeld and Nicolson, 1966). A full and well-illustrated account of Greek political development 800-400 BC.

Hart, John, *Herodotus and Greek History* (Croom Helm, 1982). This lively and readable book has a chapter on the Athenian nobility.

Hurwit, Jeffrey M., *The Art and Culture of Early Greece, 1100-480 BC* (Cornell University Press, 1985). Full and detailed art history, with plenty of social and political comment interwoven. Lively style, with good illustrations.

Jeffery, L.H., *Archaic Greece: The City-States c.700-500 BC* (Methuen, 1976). A detailed and thorough account of all the Greek states during this period, with a full bibliography and references to the original sources.

Lawrence, A.W., *Greek Architecture* (Penguin, 4th ed. 1983). A thorough survey of all aspects of this subject.

Moore, J.M., *Aristotle and Xenophon on Democracy and Oligarchy* (Chatto and Windus, 1983). Includes a translation of the *Constitution of Athens*, with a detailed commentary.

Murray, O., *Early Greece* (Fontana, 1980). A wide-ranging history of Greece from early times down to 480 BC. Good bibliography.

Parke, H.W., *Festivals of the Athenians* (Thames and Hudson, 1977). A detailed account of the development and rituals of all the festivals which the Athenians celebrated, with a calendar of the religious year.

Rhodes, P.J., *A Commentary on the Aristotelian Athenaion Politeia* (Oxford, 1981). A full and detailed commentary on the *Constitution of Athens*.

Snodgrass, A., *Archaic Greece: The Age of Experiment* (Dent, 1980). A general survey of this period, with many imaginative insights, and with particular emphasis on the archaeological evidence.

Woodford, S., *An Introduction to Greek Art* (Duckworth, 1986). A very readable and imaginative introduction, with good illustrations.

Wycherley, R.E., *The Stones of Athens* (Princeton, 1978). A readable introduction to the buildings in Athens with good coverage of the Archaic period and its problems.